First Knowledges for younger readers

Design & Building on Country

Alison Page & Paul Memmott

Illustrations by Blak Douglas

First published in Australia in 2024 by Thames & Hudson Australia
Wurundjeri Country, 132A Gwynne Street, Cremorne, Victoria 3121

Design & Building on Country © Thames & Hudson Australia 2024

Text © Alison Page and Paul Memmott 2024
Illustrations © Blak Douglas 2024

27 26 25 24   5 4 3 2 1

The moral rights of the authors and illustrator have been asserted.

All rights reserved. No part of this publication may be reproduced or transmitted in any form or by any means, electronic or mechanical, including photocopy, recording or any other information storage or retrieval system, without prior permission in writing from the publisher.

ISBN 978-1-76076-356-5
ISBN 978-1-76076-410-4 (ebook)

A catalogue record for this book is available from the National Library of Australia

Front cover: Illustration by Blak Douglas, designed by Nada Backovic
Design: Nada Backovic
Editing: Melissa-Jane Fogarty
With thanks to Nina Ross and Reconciliation Australia for editorial advice
Printed and bound in China by 1010 Printing International Limited

Thames & Hudson Australia wishes to acknowledge that Aboriginal and Torres Strait Islander peoples are the first storytellers of this nation and the Traditional Custodians of the land on which we live and work. We acknowledge their continuing culture and pay respect to Elders past and present.

thamesandhudson.com.au

Aboriginal and Torres Strait Islander peoples are advised that this book contains the names and images of people who have passed away.

Torres Strait Islanders are an integral part of the country we now call Australia. However, this book is mostly restricted to a focus on Aboriginal culture based on the authors' areas of expertise.

The stories in this book are shared with the permission of the original Aboriginal storytellers.

A note on language: There are a lot of different Aboriginal and Torres Strait Islander languages, words and spellings for cultural concepts and people groups. We have used the preferred words and spellings of the authors.

This book is dedicated not only to all teachers and students, but also to the 'Old People', the Aboriginal Elders who taught us about Country and their first knowledges, and to the next generation of designers, architects, engineers and town planners – both Aboriginal and non-Aboriginal – who are creating a more sustainable future for all Australians.

Contents

Welcome   *vii*

Chapter 1: Objects and Country   1
Chapter 2: First Nations' materials and spirituality   19
Chapter 3: Tools for living on Country   37
Chapter 4: Kitchen on Country   57
Chapter 5: The first engineers on Country   79
Chapter 6: Setting up a camp   91
Chapter 7: Building a shelter   103
Chapter 8: Aboriginal architecture today   111
Chapter 9: Design futures   129

About the creators   *136*
Important words and concepts   *139*
Index   *142*

Welcome

Aboriginal people have lived on this continent we now call Australia for over 65,000 years, and we're still counting. That means that we have the longest continuing culture in the world.

But the colonisers who arrived 250 years ago looked down upon the lifestyle of Aboriginal people. They thought that Aboriginal people were primitive. They didn't recognise the amazing houses and buildings Aboriginal people built, or their science, technology and design knowledge.

Well, they were wrong! To tell this story, designer and artist Alison Page from the Dharawal and Yuin Nations teamed up with the anthropologist Paul Memmott, who is also an architect and an environmentalist.

Together they have written a remarkable book that will show you what skilled builders and designers we are.

Margo Ngawa Neale

Chapter 1:
Objects and Country

What do you think of when you think of your country? How do you see your place in the world? Do you know what Country is?

We are going to take you deep into the Aboriginal concept of 'Country' and show how it is a way of seeing and relating to the world. We explain how Country is a place of deep knowledge and kinship. This knowledge of Country supports everything that is necessary for survival, including how to find food and water, how to protect yourself and how to find shelter. But it goes much further than that. Who you are, what you think and what you do are all part of your relationship to your Country.

You will learn the difference between just being 'on country' and 'on Country' – that's Country with a capital C. That means the full Aboriginal belief about Country that involves its spiritual nature and how the Old People thought of it as their family or kin.

What is Country?

When you meet, hear or read about an Aboriginal person, they like to include the name of the particular part of the country they are connected to, or where their Ancestors come from if they know this. Country is part of a person's identity and where their knowledge comes from. It is therefore most precious to Aboriginal people.

If you look up an Aboriginal map of the Australian continent (you can see it on the next page), you will see that it is made up of many different Countries (sometimes called nations). There are many more Aboriginal nations than there are federal states and territories of modern Australia.

Alison says

Country is a place of knowledge. It holds all the information that you need to know to live and live well. This knowledge includes all the subject areas that we study today, like the human and natural sciences and skills useful to society – law, medicine, botany, astronomy and many other areas. You name it, Aboriginal people got it first by understanding their Country.

So, if Country holds all the knowledge then Country is very, very clever!

There are over 250 Aboriginal Nations across the continent we now call Australia. Each Nation has its own cultural traditions and languages.

Connection to Country

For Aboriginal people, Country is not just a place. It is a whole way of seeing the world. Country is all around us, and it is about more than just the ground. There is Land, Sea and Sky Country too.

In the Aboriginal and Torres Strait Islander worldview there is no separation between people and nature. Everything that is on Earth, as well as the skies and the waterways, is part of Country and is a living being that is related to you. That includes all the animals, birds, fish and insects as well as the people of the past and present. It also includes the plants, the rocks and even the soil, the water and the air itself. That's why Aboriginal and Torres Strait Islander peoples know how important it is to have a connection to Country.

It is a big responsibility to know your Country. You should treat the different parts of Country like family members. So, it is as important to know your Country as it is to know who your family is, who your relations are and what they do. And just as a person must show respect for their Elders – who are the Knowledge Holders and teachers in the community – Country is there for us and needs to be respected.

It is important to care for Country and listen to your Country as you listen to and learn from family members. In return, Country will care for you.

Knowledge through Songlines

Unlike lots of other cultures, First Nations people never had the written word. They record everything in spoken stories – all the knowledge needed to survive, about animals and plants, the shape of the land and its climate, weather patterns, how to catch or find food and almost everything that you might need to know to go on living on Country. They encode this knowledge into stories, paintings, music and dance so people remember it. This connects plants, animals and places on the land and in the sky, making threads of knowledge called Songlines.

The Dreaming

In the Aboriginal worldview, everything starts and ends with Country. There are no beginnings and no endings. Everything is part of an endless flow of life and ideas coming from Country, which we also know as the Dreaming. There are different words for Dreaming in different Aboriginal languages: for example, Altyerre in Arrernte (Alice Springs), Tjukurrpa in Warlpiri (Yuendumu), Wukuna in Warumungu (Tennant Creek), Ritjinguthinha in Kalkadoon (Mount Isa) and Kuwalkujin in Lardil (Mornington Island).

You can look up the places where these languages are spoken on a map.

Certain designs and stories come from the Dreaming and are based on the experience of living and being on Country. An Aboriginal person may have a close bond, or totemic relationship, with, for example, a species of tree, or the kangaroo, or the barramundi. They can feel the spirit energies of that Ancestral Being inside them. They believe this Ancestral Being is their Ancestor too. When a human dies, their spirit also returns into the landscape as a spiritual being that might be in the form of an animal, bird or plant. Their world is alive with Ancestral Beings that are seen and unseen to this day.

When the earth, rocks, seas and skies were being created, the Ancestral Beings were like the stem cells of Country. These Ancestral Heroes put bits of themselves over the places that they made or even just touched as they passed through. These bits and pieces, including body parts, blood and bones, helped to create sites in Country and can still be seen today as maps or tracings of their journeys. Their energies or spiritual essences are still there in Country, for those who know how to read, see and feel them.

Creating Country

The Ancestral Heroes that made Country were super beings like superheroes on a creation adventure that left a path of creation (and sometimes destruction). They were the original shapeshifters that came from a time when Country was 'soft' and in formation. They 'jumped' or 'rose' up to make the rocks, cliffs and mountains, or 'opened up' to form the waterholes, rivers and oceans. These super beings not only changed their own shape, but also shaped the Country as they travelled through it. The tracks they left behind them are the Songlines.

Objects on Country

The things that are made on Country and get used on Country are also part of Country. These objects that are created become part of the Dreaming. When an Aboriginal person carves, weaves, paints or sculpts something from Country, they are channelling the spirit of their Ancestors. This comes from the stories and materials from Country, and the Ancestors who passed down their craft and left the images and designs to work with. The materials and techniques used in making all kinds of symbolic and useful objects are part of the knowledge that comes from the Ancestors and from Country.

The objects and the materials used on Country capture the energy of the place in which they are made and the Ancestors in charge of those places. People tell stories and sing songs to their objects while they make them on Country. In this way, they continue the conversation with their Ancestors from the time of the Dreaming.

Country is the source of life. It is also a place to live, a place to work, and a place to learn, as well as a place of ceremony. When you are on Aboriginal land, you might be on ceremonial grounds and you should show respect.

Many ceremonies must be performed with the proper object or design and in the right place and the right people being there.

Ceremony and song

In an exhibition at the National Museum of Australia you can see a short film about an old man called Frank Gurrmanamana from Djunawunya in Arnhem Land. Frank is making a fish trap. While he makes it, he sings it into life and talks to it as his Fish Trap Ancestor. He describes the fishing sites that the Ancestors made on Country, drawing on the power of the fish trap Ancestors to make his trap. It is a ceremony, a meaningful conversation with his object where he can remember all the fishing knowledge and what the trap will be used for on Country. As he makes it, Frank becomes it. It is his Dreaming. The object becomes like a living person.

Taken from Country

Objects made on Country are filled with ceremony. Many of these sacred objects have been collected and can be found in museums today. But for Aboriginal people, it is sad to see a treasured object far away from the Country it belongs to. These tools and objects are living beings themselves, so they long for their community and their homelands.

Chapter 2:
First Nations' materials and spirituality

A rich material culture

Connecting to Country is about understanding which materials are available to provide shelter, food, string and ropes, tools and medicines. That understanding is deeply rooted in how people relate to and can organise everything in the landscape. This means keeping on top of family and kinship networks, as well as the Songlines and the Dreamings, which give a person their totems and let them know what they can use, and how and when they can use it.

These relationships are described in great detail – on a need-to-know basis – in the stories that have been passed down person-to-person. It is important to look after and build on these relationships to keep ancestral knowledge alive.

The life cycle of Country

Country includes the built environment and all the objects that you use. Anything made from the trees, grass, earth and rocks on Country is part of Country. And when a building is pulled down, or the things you use get damaged or worn out, they go back into Country.

This also means that nothing goes to waste. Long before we learnt to put out the recycling bins and use eco-materials, Aboriginal people were using natural, sustainable materials that break down on return to the soil. Just like a person, the whole life cycle of your objects is important. They aren't just landfill to be dumped out of sight and out of mind on someone else's Country!

Paul says

Lardil man Jackson Jacob from Mornington Island was a famous maker of boomerangs. A film called *Boomerang* made for the Australian Museum provides a fascinating account of him as a master craftsman at work.

In it, he is filmed making a comeback (returning) boomerang. He is shown cutting and shaping the wood, before charring it in a fire after which he scrapes off several layers with a knife to slim the tool down further.

He then spends a lot of time heating the boomerang in the fire and then twisting its two 'legs' in opposite directions to perfect the aerodynamic design.

But, for me, the most amazing part of the film is when Jackson is shown cutting a raw piece of wood from the lower trunk of a kurrburu tree (*Acacia alleniana*) and talking to the tree. He says, 'When I do this I have to sing to the tree, to the old spirit in the tree, to say I'm sorry for cutting out a piece of him; but then his spirit will remain inside the boomerang.'

A working relationship to Country

Aboriginal people know how to tread lightly on the earth without causing damage to it. They respect their Country, taking seriously the responsibility to look after its precious material resources.

In some parts of Country, the old soils – these fine, delicate soils, some rich in mineral elements – require a light touch. This means taking from Country more sparingly than the intensive farming practices that the colonists brought with them.

Australia's unique flora and fauna have evolved over time in the different regions of the continent. These areas vary a lot between the wet and the dry and other conditions based on the climate and weather patterns there. In each of these micro-climates, natural rhythms and cycles determine what lives there and what grows there and in what seasons.

Knowledge of Country shared through the stories held in the Songlines is detailed and layered, taking into account the seasons and the life cycles of related living things that might be found in a particular part of the world at a particular time of year.

It is a working relationship based on familiarity, knowledge and respect. And that means talking to Country, listening to Country and sometimes asking permission of Country when there is the need to take from it. Have you, or someone you know, ever apologised to a plant or tree before taking a piece out of it?

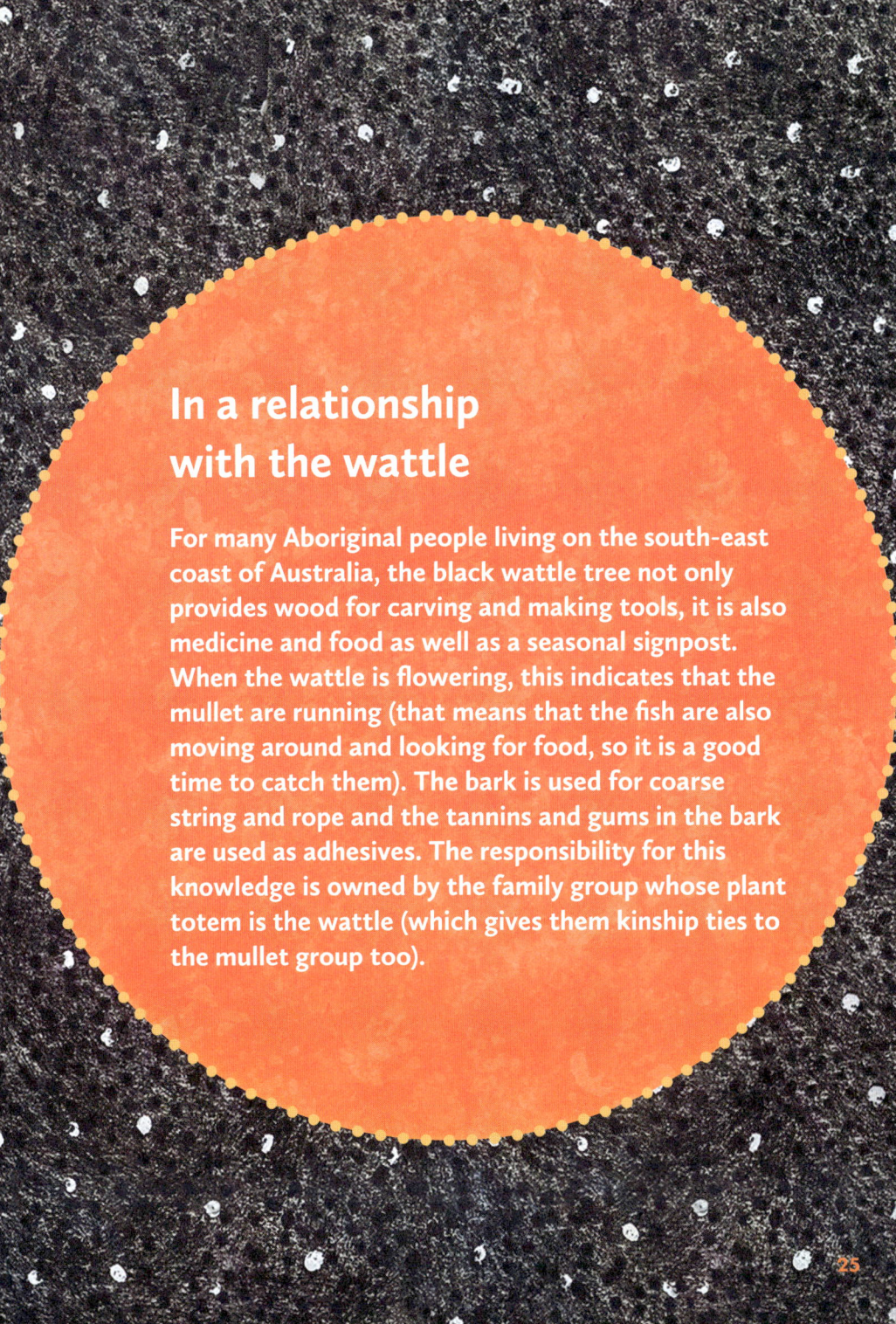

In a relationship with the wattle

For many Aboriginal people living on the south-east coast of Australia, the black wattle tree not only provides wood for carving and making tools, it is also medicine and food as well as a seasonal signpost. When the wattle is flowering, this indicates that the mullet are running (that means that the fish are also moving around and looking for food, so it is a good time to catch them). The bark is used for coarse string and rope and the tannins and gums in the bark are used as adhesives. The responsibility for this knowledge is owned by the family group whose plant totem is the wattle (which gives them kinship ties to the mullet group too).

Paul says

Lardil Elder Henry Peters Wunhun (which means beach oak) has kindly given me permission to share the part of his story that connects the boomerang to the travels of the Rainbow Serpent, which is also a great lesson in life.

At the time of creation, the kurrburu tree grew from the ribs of Thuwathu, the Rainbow Serpent in the Dreaming. Thuwathu was originally human and came to Gununa (Mornington Island) from the mainland with members of his family at the end of the dry season. They made a camp of windbreaks on the south side of the island in the hot dusty weather. But, rather than build a wungkurr (windbreak), Thuwathu chose to build a ngampirr (an enclosed shelter with walls and a roof). His family made fun of him as the wet season had not started. But within a few days a big storm came over the island. Thuwathu went into his warm, dry shelter. But his family were caught out in the wind and the torrential monsoon rain. They were not prepared for the wet weather and didn't have enough firewood.

Thuwathu's sister Bulthuku (Willy Wagtail) was particularly upset because her newborn baby was shivering and sneezing and before long the baby had an unhealthy 'hotness' (a high temperature). She went to the door of Thuwathu's ngampirr three or four times to ask him if she could put her baby in his shelter. She could see through the gap between the walls that there was enough space. But each time, he said, 'No, sister, go away. That space is for my knee' (or arm or head or foot).

The baby died and Bulthuku was so sad and angry that she lit Thuwathu's ngampirr with a firestick and he was burnt alive inside.

The building burnt down and Thuwathu came out with his skin looking like charcoal. In agony, he crawled through the Country, twisting and turning, and carved out a riverbed (Dugong River). As he travelled, his ribs broke out and stuck in the ground, becoming the kurrburu trees. Then Thuwathu became the Rainbow Serpent, living in the sea around the Wellesley Islands.

Alison says

Dean Kelly, a Yuin man who is a ranger with the NSW National Parks and Wildlife Service, gave me some useful advice about how to ask permission from a tree.

He taught me to stand in front of the tree or bush and place my bare feet on the ground, tell the bush I am coming and that I am here to ask if I can take these leaves. When you are deeply connected to Country and able to listen, you will hear the answer to the question. It may be 'No', in which case you have to find another tree that is willing to give.

Materials made from plants

A lot of the world's most useful materials come from the many different types of plants on the many different types of Country. Trees of hard and soft wood, as well as shrubs, bushes, canes, roots, grasses, reeds and lichens, provide rich material and renewable resources for almost every human need. That includes food, medicine and a big range of lightweight tools, equipment and building materials.

Following are some common examples of multi-purpose, super-useful, plant-based materials.

The many uses of a sheet of bark

Bark can be easily cut or stripped from trees and can be used for a variety of purposes. Bark can be very flexible and strong as well as easily shaped or bent and cut into regular sizes like factory-made building materials. Sheets of bark come in many different sizes, thicknesses and qualities, ranging from the flat, stiff and stringy eucalyptus bark to the lighter, softer and easier to shape melaleuca paperbark.

Large bark sections were used to make canoes and shelters. They sometimes needed to be combined with grass string or rope to hold the bits together and sealed with clay, gums and resins for waterproofing. Bark was also good for other things, like mats, raised floors, ledges and bedding material. People used it to serve and wrap food, as a cover for baking things, for bandaging flesh wounds or for carrying water. Bark cloaks and dancing hats were often worn in ceremonies, and a bark torch was a useful tool to light the way at night or to carry fire.

Building with bark

Bark technology was used for walls and roofs to protect people from the sun, rain and wind or to keep warm in cold weather. First Nations people were so skilled at making bark shelters that some of the first colonists borrowed, copied or stole Aboriginal bark shelters and lean-tos, the designs and the homes themselves, adapting traditional Indigenous housing design for their own use. And some colonists paid Aboriginal people for bark sheets at markets and some employed Aboriginal people to build their cottages out of poles and bark.

The organic hardware store

The many different types of bark, grasses and other fibres were twisted together to make string, twine or rope. It would be enough to fill an entire aisle of a hardware store today! It is hard to think of more useful materials that were adapted to join, fasten and weave things. Strong hand-twisted fibre lengths are particularly good for making into nets to catch fish, insects, birds and animals on Country. Human hair was used for making men's belts. You can read more about the amazing designs for traps, bags and baskets using handmade strings and beach vines in chapter 4.

Uses of spinifex

Spinifex is an especially useful and hardy grass that is used for weaving things and as a waterproof roof covering. Many Aboriginal groups knew a lot about the special properties of the sticky resin from spinifex. It was used in some medicines and as a type of gum or glue to fix and seal the wrapping joining the stone blade to a wooden handle for a spear, knife or chisel.

If you want to know more about the amazing nano-properties that Aboriginal people discovered in spinifex grass, go to chapter 5.

BUNGAREES
ORGANIC hardware
OCHRE / TWINE / BARK
BLACK
RED
WHITE
BLOODWOOD
SCRIBBLY BK.
IRON WOOD

Separation from Country

Very few Aboriginal and Torres Strait Islander communities have been able to live a traditional life on Country that was not interrupted by the colonists or the unjust and racist policies of Australian state and federal governments. These policies led to many people being separated and disconnected from their people and their Country.

By the mid-20th century, only small groups of people living in very remote or island communities were able to avoid being removed from their lands and resettled into Aboriginal missions and reserves. The Lardil from the Wellesley Islands were one group who avoided being removed from their lands. They were one of the last Queensland groups to practise string-making continuously. They were experts in string, rope and net manufacturing.

Different types of Country

The type of Country you live on also becomes part of your identity and your material culture. For example, some people are desert people and some people are saltwater people. The material elements of nature are what defines you and your Dreamings and much of what you do on your Country. Aboriginal people often say that they are from 'freshwater' or 'saltwater' Country to distinguish between the two types of waters.

There are places where freshwater and saltwater stream together. One special place for both freshwater and saltwater people was the headland on which the Sydney Opera House stands today. This was where the freshwater rivers and streams flowed into the harbour before heading out into the Pacific Ocean. The Traditional Owners of the land called it Tubowgule/Dubbagullee.

At Tubowgule the crushed shells from shell beds and some middens were used as the lime slurry for the cement mortar in the foundations and walls of the first colonial buildings in Sydney, so the material memory of this site was overwritten by the British colonists.

34

Alison says

The British colonists renamed Tubowgule several times. First they called it Cattle Point, as this was a key source of food for them. Later they renamed it Limeburners' Point, after the cement. Then they named it Bennelong Point after an Aboriginal man who became a kind of ambassador, as he communicated between his people and the British governors. But none of the names they gave it reflected the true meaning of the place for the Traditional Owners who lived and gathered there for hundreds, if not thousands, of years. They had nothing to do with the traditional Aboriginal name, meaning 'where the knowledge waters meet'.

The knowledge about how to crush the shells and release the lime to bind stone and bricks for building was something that my people did get to use. When I was very young, I would camp on the south coast with my extended family over weeks in the summer. One year all it did was rain, day after day, turning our campsite to mud and water. My aunties collected shells in buckets and crushed the shells, adding spit and water until they made a basic form of concrete that they laid underneath our tents so we could stay longer that year.

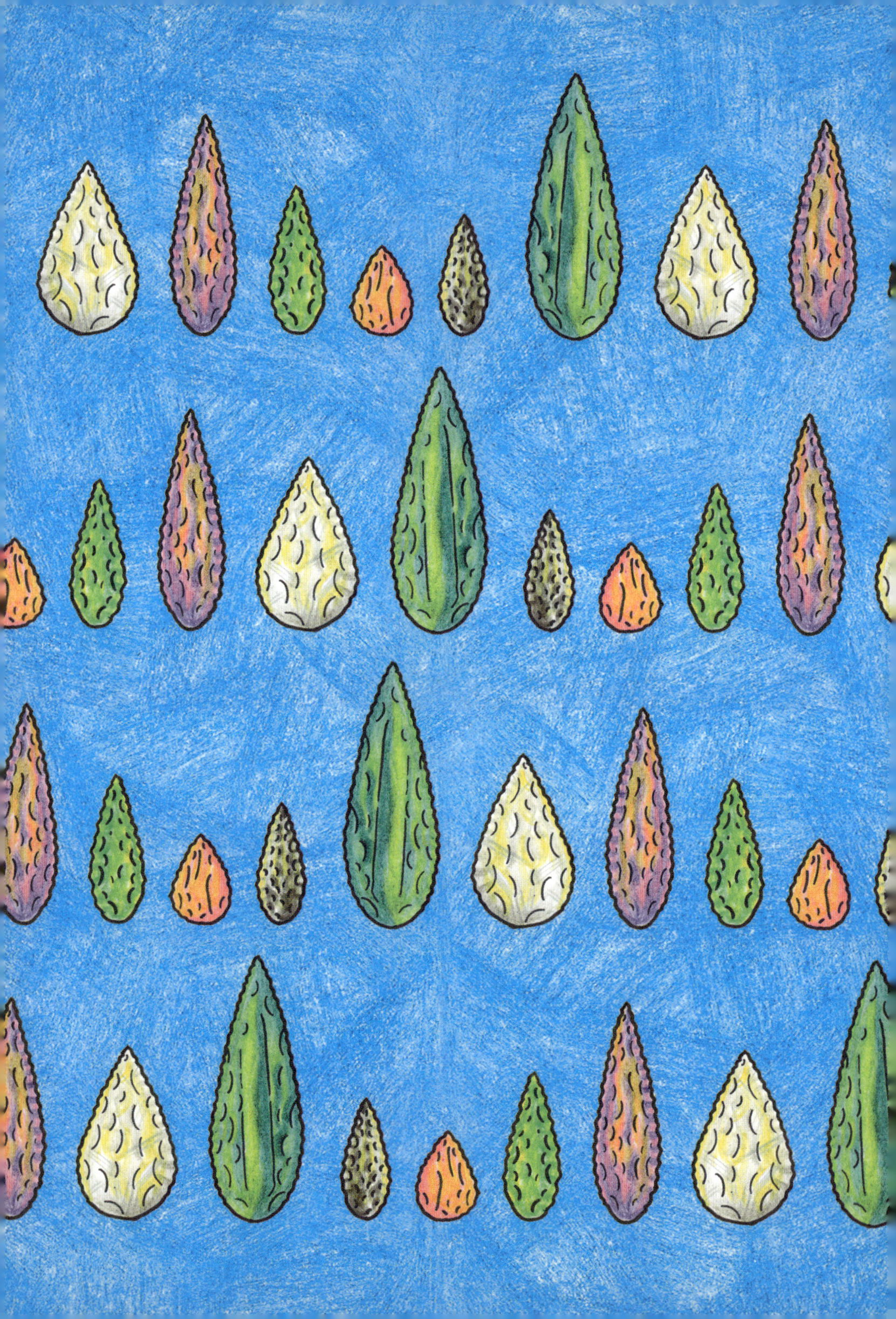

Chapter 3:
Tools for living on Country

Aboriginal people adapted to live in a very flexible and mobile way, depending on the type of Country they were connected to. Desert people were more likely to travel further within their territories to find food, water and materials for their tools and equipment. People living in the tropical North, where there is high rainfall and more vegetation, were more likely to set up a semi-permanent camp and stick to a smaller area. People visited certain parts of their Country at particular times of year when food was plentiful and when responsibility for ceremonies and group get-togethers took them there. These get-togethers were also a time to trade tools and artefacts and share stories and cultural knowledge, including the best ways of making and doing things.

Following in the footsteps of their Ancestors from the Dreaming, people travelled in all directions to get what they needed. A particular type of tool or material might not always be available locally and so had to be imported. And, just like the expensive designer items manufactured in other countries that we buy today (like Italian leather shoes), these much-travelled tools and materials had a special status. They were valued for their quality and usefulness but even more so if they had been produced with a special song by their maker or contained the spirit of an Ancestral Being.

Wherever a prized tool or artefact goes, it is often accompanied by its Dreaming story.

Some examples of material culture on the move include the red ochre from the ochre (or coloured clay) quarries near Parachilna in Adnyamathanha Country in the Flinders Ranges of South Australia. It made its way north to the Georgina River trade route, passing around Kati Thanda-Lake Eyre and all the way to central-west Queensland. A similar journey was made with the most prized obsidian (a volcanic green glass) from western Victoria that was ideal for making sharp knives and spearheads.

Similarly, the young men of Central Australia wore decorated shell pendants to mark their initiation into manhood. These dazzling new accessories were obtained for them through the trade routes that went inland from Broome and the Gulf of Carpentaria, linking coastal groups with desert nations.

39

Stone tools on Country

Stone tools have been found on beaches and deserts all over the continent, far away from where they were made on Country. These stone objects have many stories to tell of where they started and where they ended up. They also give us useful information about the histories and cultures of Aboriginal peoples and what they did, including knowledge about trade routes that cross the country sometimes thousands of miles along waterways.

To Aboriginal peoples still living on Country these stone tools are not just museum objects of archaeological value. These objects are in a relationship with the Ancestral Beings who first invented, made and used them. They channel the stories of

Alison says

Some people say that First Nations peoples already knew about quantum theory and particle physics when they talked about energy waves coming from rocks. I learnt from the Native American Blackfoot people that the knowledge of many First Peoples is up there with the more recent advances in Western science. And when we examine our kinship systems, we can see they contain complex mathematics.

In general, Aboriginal peoples are more connected to the natural world. Their respect for all living things is what has helped them to continually advance their knowledge.

their creation as the places where ceremonies were held, countless songs sung and dances performed. They also become part of the family and the kinship system of those living descendants who still carry the knowledge with them.

Each new generation of toolmakers takes on the role of looking after their Country as they learn the skills required to continue their material cultural traditions. Some of their stories are told here.

Paul says

I spent much time with the Indjilandji people from the Barkly Tableland around Lake Francis and the Georgina River at Camooweal in central-west Queensland in the 1990s. They told me how they got the stone tools they needed. Some of these were imported and some they could make themselves.

There is no sandstone where the Indjilandji people live. So large, flat slabs of sandstone that they needed for grindstone bases had to be imported from the Wangkamanha people of the Toko Range. That is some 300 kilometres to the south-west on the eastern edge of the Simpson Desert.

Greenstone axes made from an igneous (volcanic) rock were also in demand, as the Indjilandji people liked to use them for chopping into trees to extract the much-loved honey of the wild bees, or for breaking out timber slabs used for making boomerangs from acacia trees. These axes came from the Kalkadunga people in the highlands near Mount Isa. The Kalkadunga were stonemason specialists, as there were plenty of igneous and metamorphic rocks in their area.

The Indjilandji people made some of their own stone-cutting tools from a fine-grained rock known as ribbon stone that was on their Country. This stone is good for knapping (shaping) into blades of various shapes and sizes that can be used as meat-butchering knives, spearheads, chisels and also surgical tools. Chisel blades were good for cutting and shaving down timber shields and coolamons (carrying vessels) and making special grooved boomerangs. But the blades often needed replacing as they blunted quickly. So, the people kept with them a bag of spares, as well as a supply of spinifex gum for gluing the blade to a wooden handle.

I had the memorable opportunity to travel on Country with a master Indjilandji stonemason and community Elder, Colin Saltmere Pwerle. He knew where to find the best quality stones that with a few small blows of a hammerstone could be split into the perfect blade. On this trip we came across a pure white outcrop of fine chert ribbon stone that appeared above the ground in small sections along a 50-kilometre ridge that stretched far into the distance. But Colin's ancestral connection to this Country made him see much further than that. He was sensing a spirit in this stone that enhanced its quality and value to his people.

43

Lost tools and objects of Country

Many of the earliest known wooden tools, weapons and other artefacts by First Nations peoples are held in museum collections. This is in contrast to those ancient stone knives, points or blades that remain on the deserts and beaches; these types of material culture are more likely to be impacted by the passing of time and the wear and tear of use. Left on Country, the museum artefacts made from wood, plant fibres and other organic substances would have been part of the cycle of life and most likely have long since returned to the earth. Aboriginal peoples would say that 'They have gone back into Country' or 'They have returned to Country'.

That means if you want to know more about the history of the rich material cultural heritage of Aboriginal peoples, you might have to travel all over the world to view these orphaned objects that have been bought, traded or stolen by the early colonists and explorers, missionaries, anthropologists, tourists and collectors. Often these historical objects are not correctly documented and labelled, and it can be years (if at all!) before the connections can be made with their Traditional Owners that mean the objects might be returned to Country.

Many First Nations peoples throughout the globe believe return (or repatriation) of objects back to their homelands and communities is a moral right, and museums have a responsibility to reconnect peoples with their cultural heritage. But in Australia, as in many Pacific Island nations, we are fortunate to have knowledge of continuing cultural traditions on Country, and a raft of Aboriginal and non-Aboriginal researchers working to restore the cultural knowledge so that we don't lose any more of it.

Boomerangs, spears and woomeras

As with all tools made on Country, the types of boomerangs, clubs, spears and spearthrowers (called woomeras) were crafted to suit the culture, landscape and variety of animals that lived there.

Desert people were more likely to go after big game (large animals) like kangaroo, wallaby, emu and different types of reptiles (perenties, pythons), but saltwater people were more likely to hunt crocodiles, turtles and dugongs (also known as sea cows) as well as large schools of fish, using a variety of techniques to corner, capture and spear them.

As told in the Songlines, many toolmakers and tool users are legendary, with stories to tell that pass on useful knowledge. Knowing your prey and how to make your tools for cornering, catching and carefully killing them was an essential skill. So, too, was the knowledge of your totem animal's lifestyle and habits. Respect for all your totems on Country is an essential part of your life and theirs. An Indigenous person never takes from Country more than they or their family and community can eat. There are strict rules and guidelines about who can kill or eat an animal depending on their kinship relation with it.

And no knowledgeable hunter went anywhere without a kit bag of the essential tools, just in case dinner turned up!

46

Coming back to Country

Among the first objects to be stolen by colonists in Australia were a series of spears and a shield taken by Lieutenant James Cook at Kamay (Botany Bay) after first contact with the Gweagal people in 1770. The spears were cut down to fit in the ship and have been in British institutions for 250 years. In 2024, four of the spears were returned after decades of negotiations. This was not only a big moment for the Dharawal people at La Perouse, but also for all Australians because it is starting to heal our shared history, which has some very dark chapters. Because Aboriginal people believe objects are living beings, these spears will talk and tell stories about what they witnessed at that time of the first encounters.

Alison says

The woomera (spearthrower) is a particularly useful tool. Its main purpose is to guide the spear being thrown, increasing the accuracy, power and speed of the thrust. Apart from bringing down animals, a woomera has many other uses, such as making fire, and carrying plants, seeds and other collectable goods. Many woomeras are made with a stone blade attached to the handle for cutting up meat and other materials. It's like the original (or Aboriginal) version of the Swiss Army knife. And knowing how to use it is a skill in itself.

The many different types of boomerangs

Boomerangs are as many and varied as the cultural groups that use them. For the Lardil people of Mornington Island, they are basically divided into three categories: the heavy throwing, clubbing and fighting boomerang (juluwarr) that is also good at bringing an animal down from a distance; the high-flying comeback boomerang for sky hunting (thaankur wangal); and the hooked boomerang (mungkuburr), which is the deadliest fighting tool of them all.

A common design of a fighting boomerang is for one side to be flat and the other side more gently curved. An interesting fact about this is that one side is then more comfortably thrown by a right-handed thrower and the other by a left-handed thrower.

The Alyawarr people of Central Australia even have a Dreaming about the mighty power of left-handed throwers. It tells the story of the capture of the flying fox, Pitungu, after he stole two young women and ran off with them, wrapping their hair in his woomera and hurling them a long distance in place of a spear. But the boomerang that saved them, and stopped Pitungu in his tracks, came from a left-handed thrower, who is now celebrated for all time.

Boomerangs have many stories and many uses, and not just the obvious ones. You can use them as a tool to rake the coals of a fire, and (with two of them clapped together) they also make a musical percussion instrument. But if they are not made from the best quality hardwood, they will soon crack and break. They also don't sound as good. If an Aboriginal person was going to dance and play music with them, they knew to use the larger, heavier, fighting ones, not the lightweight ones!

Sacred designs for ceremony

The Warlpiri people from Yuendumu often painted sacred designs on their boomerangs and timber shields while they sang the Dreaming songs during ceremonies. After ceremony the designs were wiped off because the people believed that the sacred designs were too overwhelming or threatening for everyday use.

Spears are also many and varied across the continent. The Lardil fishing spear has three acacia prongs. Men stood in waist-deep salt water on sand spits, and speared large passing fish such as trevally, barracuda or barramundi, ensuring accuracy with their woomeras. The fishing spear was also inserted into rock cavities in the tidal zone to catch mud crabs. A single-pronged spear would be used for hunting land animals, while a spear with stingray barbs on the prongs might be used in a fighting duel.

Going fishing

The Lardil people ate a lot of seafood and used a large multi-pronged spear and a spearthrower when fishing.

Tools made from new materials on Country

The arrival of the British colonists had some surprising impacts on traditional Aboriginal material culture. Tools made from new materials on Country were traded and shared all around Australia after the colonists arrived. Sometimes these new materials arrived before Aboriginal people got to see a white person for themselves. By that time, they had often been thoroughly modified and adapted to new uses that were appropriate to the material cultural needs of the people of the Country. The mob must have thought Country was offering them up something new!

Sometimes these new tools and materials were an improvement on the old ways of doing things. The new materials were a great convenience. And the tools made from them could be lighter, sharper or more long-lasting. But the changes to peoples' lifestyles also caused a lot of conflict and anxiety when new ways and old ways collided.

Paul says

A stone vs a metal axe

Take one of those stone tools, like an axe of special cutting quality and strength. Such an object may be found far away from the stone Country on which it was made or traded and has become part of the family kinship structures as an ancestral object. Its rarity, function and usefulness give it a high status. For this reason, ownership of this treasured object is passed down through senior members of the community.

Then along comes a new thing, a metal axe that was gifted or traded from the new colonists on Country. It is in a class of its own for sharpness, lightness and strength. Not only does it replace that stone axe, but it also changes the traditional value because it is so much more widely available. This metal tool is one of many that can now be found all over the continent. This new metal axe changes the world order of axes forever. But, even more importantly, it changes the way people relate to one another and their ancestral objects.

This is what happened to the Yir Yoront people of the Cape York Peninsula in the 1940s when a large supply of metal axes arrived in the community. Then, many more members of the community got hold of axes – including women and boys. It was a useful tool. But it broke all the rules around who had permission to use an axe. It caused disruption to the community. And similar things were happening all around the continent.

Alison says

A boomerang with a metal collar

When builders were excavating the ground for a sewerage system in a suburban street near where I am from in La Perouse, they discovered a boomerang about 10 metres underground. This boomerang was one of the oldest found in New South Wales. It must have been a treasured belonging of one of the Traditional Owners who lived in this area that was once covered by sand dunes, not that far from where the *Endeavour* landed at Kamay (Botany Bay).

What was also curious about this particular boomerang was the way the object had been added to. A steel collar had been wrapped around its centre. The metal is a skilfully added piece of sheeting that is curled around the edges of the boomerang. It was a well-worn object with chipped edges, so the retrofitting with the stronger material would have made it last much longer.

The glass bottle that became a spearhead

In the Kimberley region of Western Australia, spearheads – also known as spearpoints – were often made from glass bottles or the ceramic insulators used on telegraph poles and phone lines. Already, by the early 19th century, these new glass-point spearheads were incredibly popular in the Kimberley.

Finely flaked glass was more easily worked than stone and was much sharper than a wooden spearhead. They were deadly when they pierced the skin, so they were prized tools for hunting. And when the spear itself broke, it was easy to replace the shaft and remount the glass spearpoint.

As the spearpoints were traded along the Songlines that started out in the Kimberley region, they also became part of the Dreaming. By the time they had got to the Central Australian and Western Desert areas, they had become symbols of lightning and rain. These visual qualities of glass – being so shiny, dazzling and see-through – clearly fascinated Aboriginal people when they first came in contact with European-style manufactured glass.

Recycling and reusing materials

Have you ever had a shoe, favourite toy or other object patched to make it last longer? It is always good to have someone in the family who knows how to fix things using the available materials. As you will read about later in chapter 8, throughout the 19th and 20th centuries, Aboriginal people living on the land and on the fringes of towns and cities knew how to put to good use new materials like canvas or fabric, wire, glass, sheet metal and corrugated iron. And they still do!

But when Aboriginal people first came across these new tools and materials, sometimes they felt troubled. These new things came at a cost to traditional values and especially to Country. They could be seen as an alien invasion, like the people who brought them here!

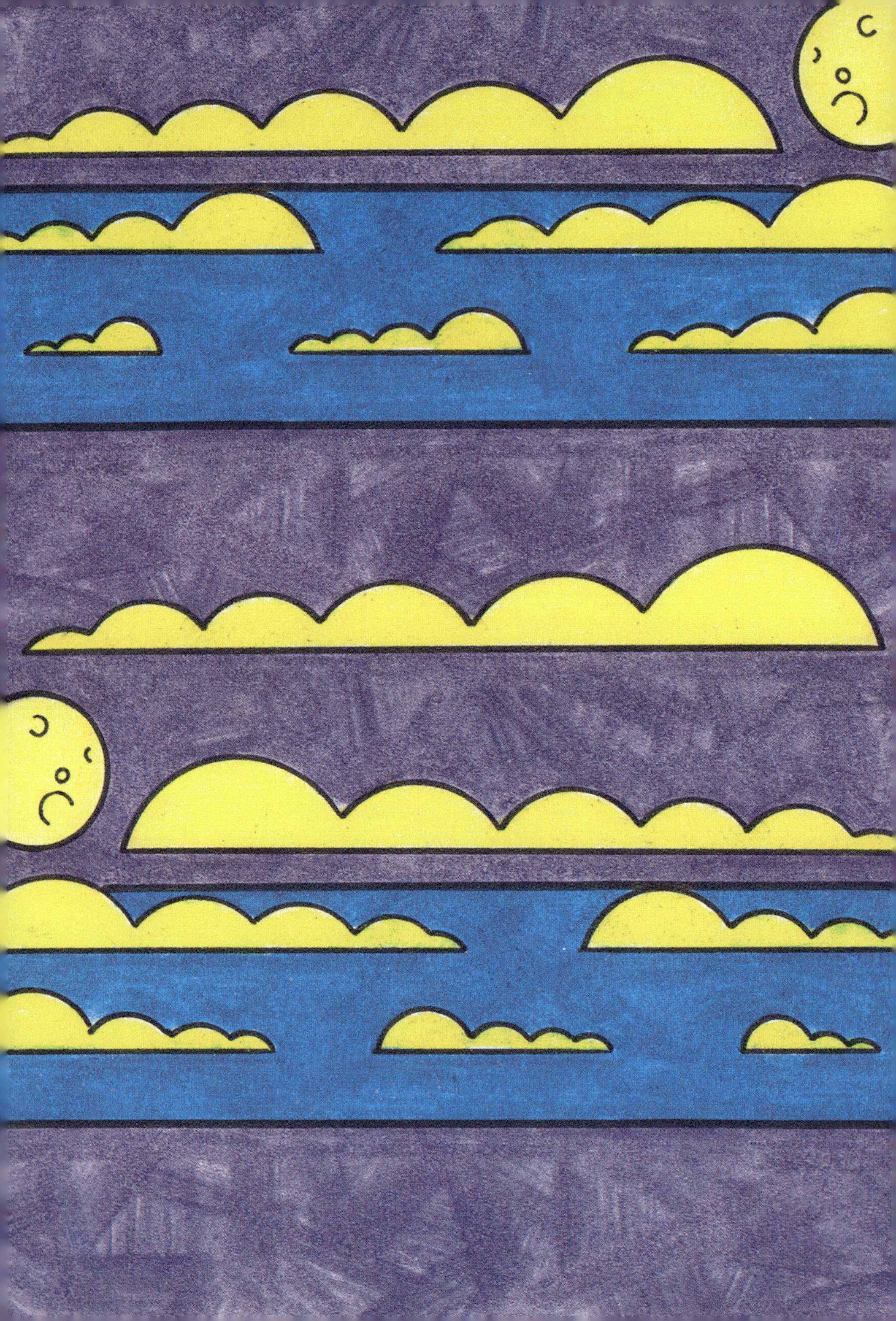

Chapter 4:
Kitchen on Country

People like to get together in times of plenty. For Aboriginal peoples, this might be a time when the bogong moths on high Country are swarming and ready to harvest; or when large runs of fish occur on the east coast (like mullet), or when the large nuts of the bonyi (bunya) pines ripen and drop. Several thousand people gathered for these big harvests.

But there were many smaller feast events too. A hunting party would be sent out to catch and kill some game like a kangaroo or a couple of wallabies, or – for those living on the coast and local waterways – a crocodile, dugong or turtle. Once caught, the animals were ready to be fired and roasted, and a messenger with a message stick sent the word out for a planned or impromptu feast. These occasions often turned into big events when everyone got to hear the news and discuss important business. Song, dance and ceremony were important parts of the event, as was settling disputes and grievances.

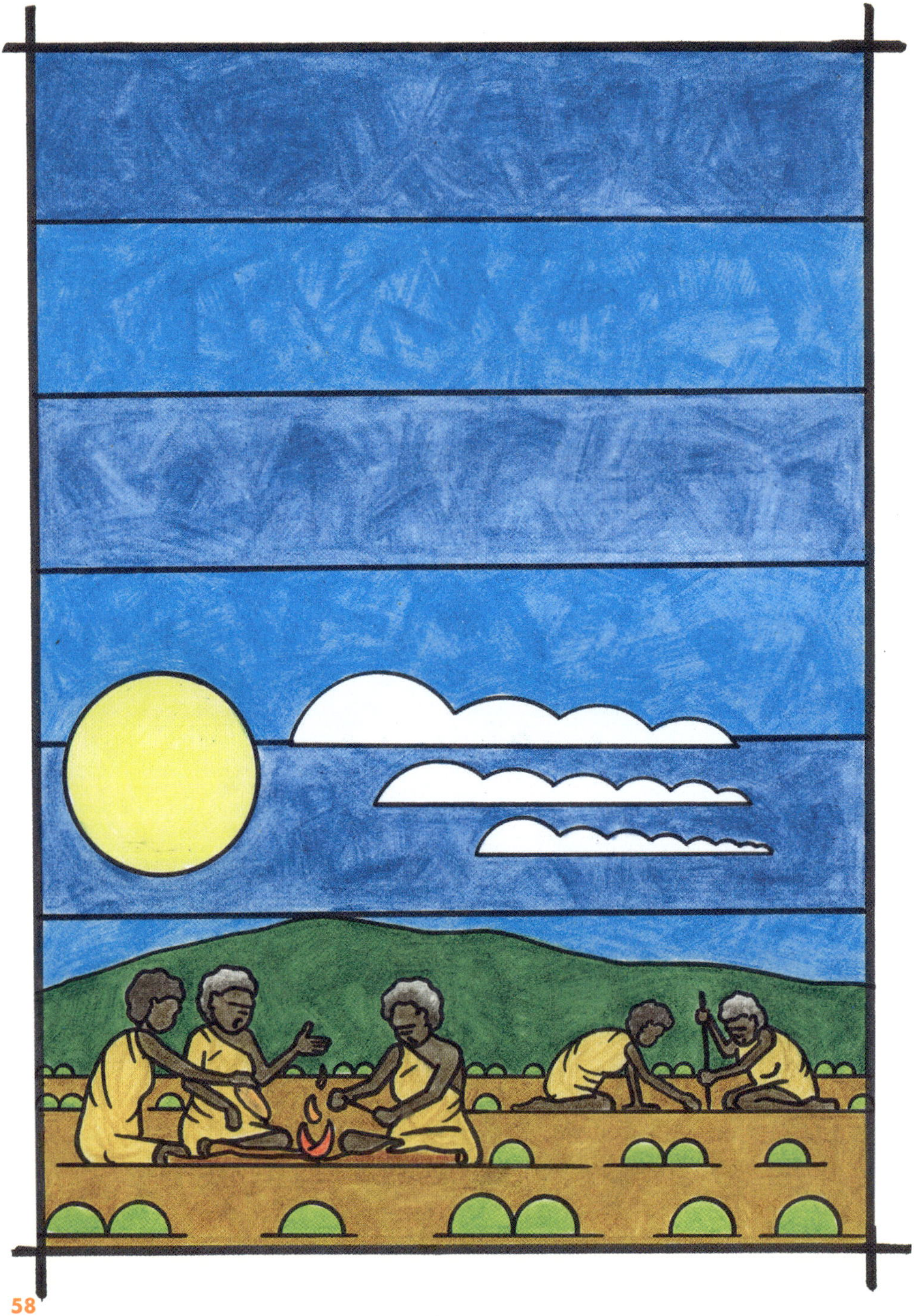

Invitation to a party

Sometimes people from the whole neighbourhood and further afield were invited by messengers to join the party, depending on how much food was available. For the very big feasts involving hundreds or thousands of people, messengers would be sent out months in advance to give time for distant peoples to travel (no mobile phones then!). But the celebration couldn't happen if there was not enough to eat and drink. Without the convenience of fridges, shops and supermarkets, feasts had to be timed around seasonal plant harvests, or big fish and animal kills. It was especially good if you could bring down a big land or sea animal. In some coastal areas up to six or more dugongs would be killed, each with as much meat as a cow.

Big game hunting was what the men did on Country. They knew their Songlines and their Dreamings about particular animals related to them. They knew about how and where the animals swam, burrowed or roamed freely on their Country and could be hunted.

The women did a lot of the food preparation work and heavy lifting, as they went to get firewood and collect loads of bush fruit and vegetables. They filled their coolamons, woven bags and bark buckets with smaller animals like mud crabs, lizards and goannas, all the while thinking respectfully of their ancestral providers and thanking Country for its provision.

Alison says
Collecting gourmet foods

Many different types of woven bags and baskets or wooden bowls called coolamons were used for collecting and carrying berries, bulbs, grains, tubers and small animals such as birds, crabs, oysters, fish, lizards, goannas and insects, including bogong moths and witchetty grubs. Some of these foods are good to eat uncooked accompanied by fresh-picked bush limes, tomatoes and other berries and fruits in season.

Paul says

Many important Aboriginal ceremonies are what anthropologists call 'increase rituals'. That means the dance, song and performance is aimed at encouraging animals, plants and humans to live and grow, increasing in their number.

The Ancestral Heroes of the Yellow Goanna men can be called on to encourage more goannas, which the people particularly liked to eat. The Goanna Dreaming had to be held at the right place on Country where the yellow goannas liked to live, their 'story place' or sacred site.

Similarly, a ceremony created by the Rain Ancestors in the Dreaming can be held at a place where the people really want it to rain. The Rain Dreaming was designed to turn on the sky tap.

Netting fish and other animals

Aboriginal peoples living on freshwater or saltwater Country were especially good at netting and trapping fish, sharks, eels, turtles and stingrays that could then be speared and pulled out of the water, and sometimes cooked and served in large numbers. Nets were also used to trap land animals, sometimes in combination with firestick farming to steer the hunted animals in the right direction, like into a corner from which they couldn't escape!

It took hours and hours of labour to make nets from bush twine or rope, and then construct them, sometimes with additional wooden poles. Depending on the size and design of the net, they often needed more than one person to work them.

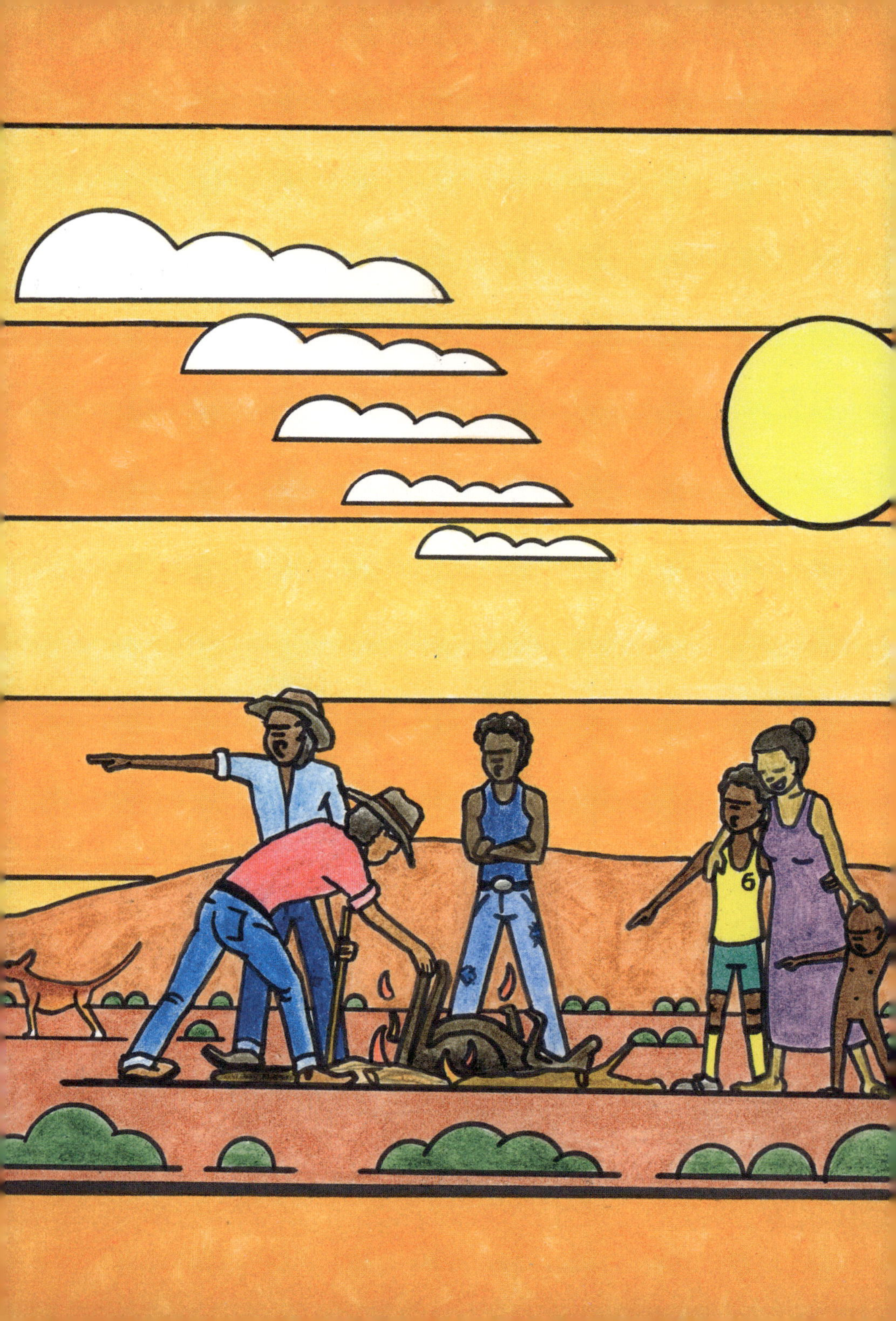

Going to the butcher shop

Big game hunters used spears, harpoons, clubs, nets and boomerangs to bring down larger animals like crocodiles, dugongs, turtles, emus, kangaroos and wallabies. To 'bring down' is the polite way of saying that these animals were killed, sometimes netted, stunned or knocked out first, before they were finished off. A stone axe, flint or shell knife was then used to skin them and remove the guts.

Have you seen an X-ray-style painting of the insides of a goanna, a kangaroo or a crocodile by the Kunwinjku people of Western Arnhem Land? These images are graphic and accurate depictions of the bones and various body parts, just like the sign in a butcher shop!

Paul says

The Lardil people made four types of fishing nets with grass string. The mijil (a hand net or purse net) was good for catching an individual fish chased from a rocky crevice. The dumunthar (elliptical scoop net) was used for catching whole schools of small fish and prawns.

The dulnhu kirra (grass-string net with wooden poles) was used for catching dulnhu or 'month fish' – they got their name because they only appeared for around one month each year.

Once the fish are in the net, the poles can be pushed together to close the mouth of the net and trap the fish inside.

They made an even larger two-handled dugong net called a barkuwen from heavier ropes made from the bark of the yellow-flowered madard (*Hibiscus tiliaceus*), also called a 'cotton tree' in coastal Queensland.

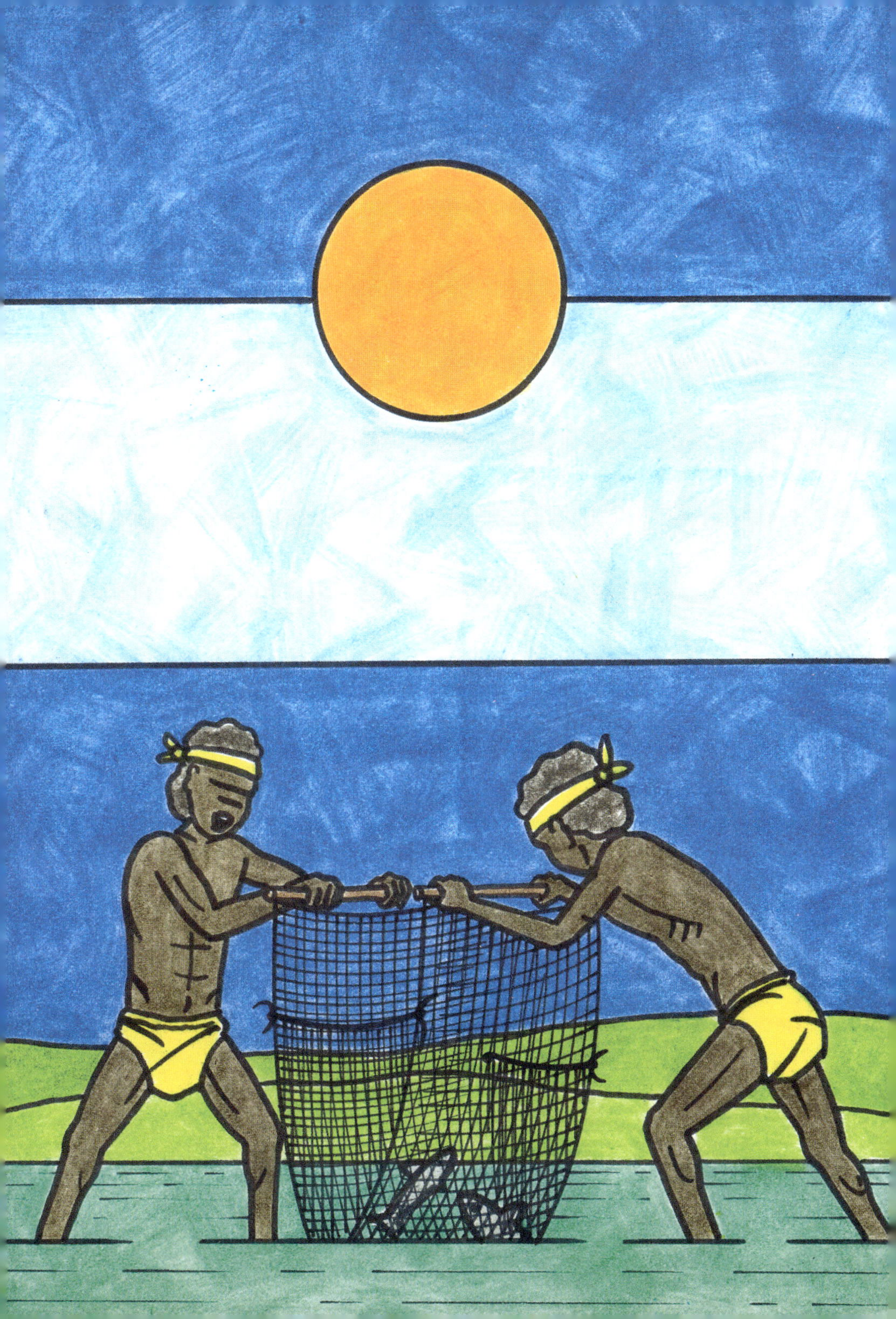

Preparing the daily bread

The food that people ate on a daily basis often needed the most preparation time. Grains and seeds from grasses, shrubs, trees and bushes were hand-picked and threshed or winnowed to separate the seeds from the rest of the plant. This could be done by hitting the plants with sticks of bark sheets, or shaking the seeds loose in a coolamon and blowing the foliage away.

Certain seeds first needed soaking or leaching of harmful substances in a sealed basket or parcel in the bed of a waterhole or creek for a week or so. The grains were prepared by crushing them down to a fine meal or powder using a stone pounder with a flat grinding stone. Then the meal was mixed with water to make a pasty substance that was kneaded into dough. The mixture could then be placed in the hot ashes of a fire for cooking.

Yams and tubers (bush potatoes) could also be cooked in hot ashes and/or made into bread. It requires a good knowledge of Country to know when it is time to harvest them, as these root vegetables grow under the ground. You might have seen women on Country with their digging sticks pulling up yams and other tubers out of the ground. When the yam daisies (murnong) from the south-eastern states were in full bloom, the people knew it was time to harvest the yams. The flowers and leaves were good to eat too!

67

Kitchen tools on Country

Aboriginal peoples have been stocking their campfire kitchens with useful tools and appliances for thousands of years. These are the traditional equivalent of the contents of today's kitchen cupboard. But, of course, these tools were portable and their materials came from particular places on Country. That's also where they got their power from!

Over the next few pages, we have given you a list of some of the most popular ones.

Some useful bowls, buckets and carry-alls

Bull kelp containers

Tasmanian Aboriginal people use the giant southern bull kelp, which is a species of seaweed, to make water containers. They are made by folding and shaping the damp kelp into the form of a basket that is filled with sand and left to dry. When the kelp dries out it hardens and becomes like leather. The container can then be used as a water carrier and drinking cup.

Bark buckets

These bark containers from the Kimberley region of Western Australia were used by Aboriginal people to collect foodstuffs

> **Alison says**
>
> When we step into a modern kitchen, it's easy to forget that the appliances we use – like a toaster, breadmaker or food processor – do the same thing that my ancestors long ago did with campfires, grinding stones, spears, stone axes, digging sticks and other tools.
>
> And archaeologists have recently discovered that Australian Aboriginal people are the world's oldest breadmakers. The grains they used were gluten free and full of nutrients. Now that's a discovery!

and carry water. They are made from sheets of bark, sewn and sealed at the seams with spinifex gum or beeswax, and decorated with ochre designs.

In certain rock art paintings from the Kimberley in Western Australia, you can see the wandjina spirit figures carrying such buckets. But these days, most people use cheap plastic ones, which don't carry with them the stories from the Dreaming.

Bicornual baskets

These mathematically perfect baskets are unique to the rainforest cultures of North Queensland. Made by both men and women from lawyer cane, gathered and stripped of its sharp hooks, they are carried on the back and held in place by woven string worn across

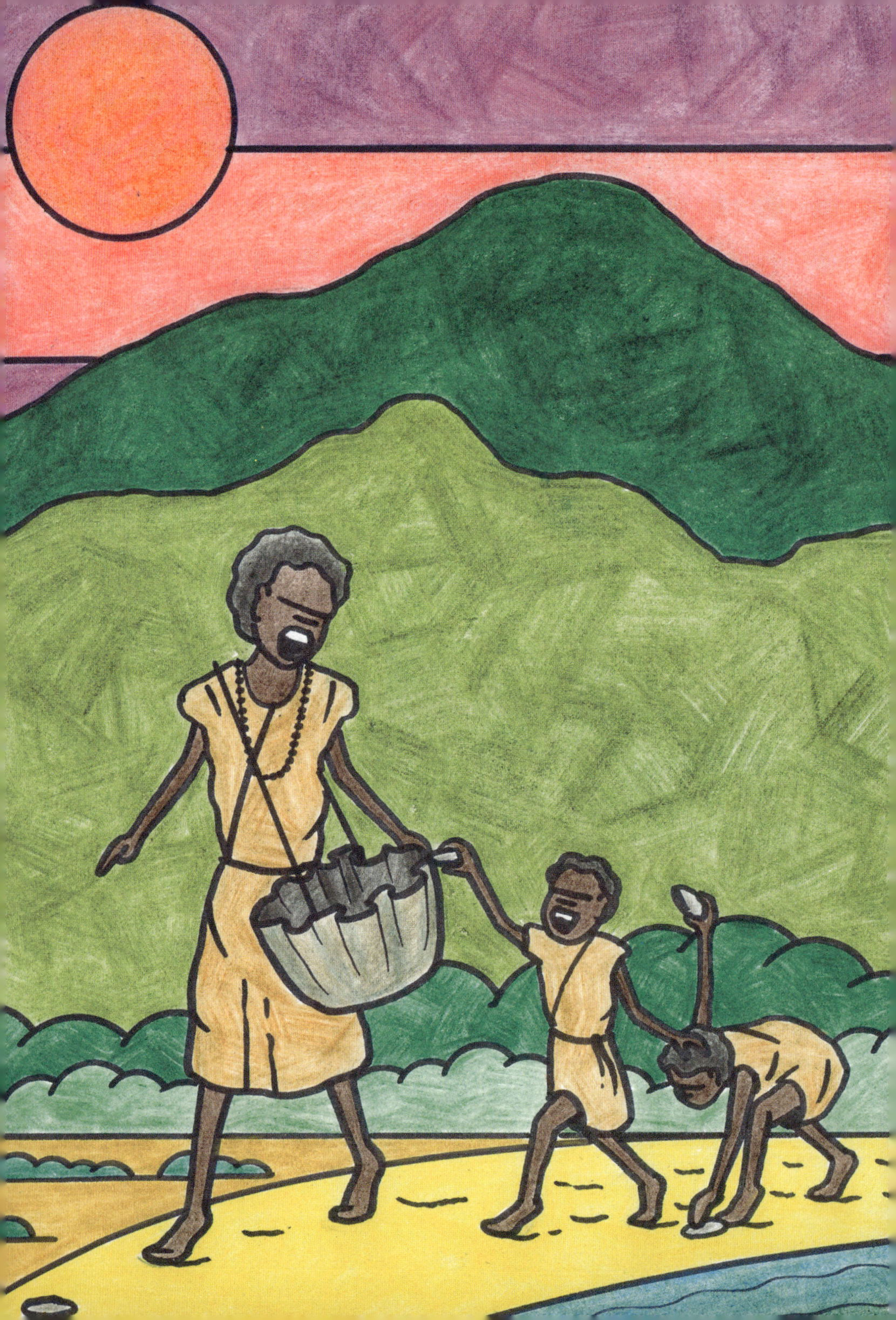

the forehead. In the past, women used them for collecting food and as baby carriers, while men used them to carry their hunting tools and for ceremonial things. Their open weave made them ideal for leaching food in running water. What a cool backpack!

Dilly bags

These round-bottomed baskets, or dilly bags, come from Arnhem Land in the Northern Territory. Woven from split pandanus fibre, these bags made by skilled women were often created with hand-dyed fibres and covered in painted ochre designs. Like the bicornual baskets, they are carried on the back and tied by a woven string worn across the forehead. This means that the wearer's hands are free for gathering food.

Coolamons

These containers, or coolamons, from the Central and Western Deserts, have many different uses, and their different shapes reflect those uses. Shallow coolamons are used for winnowing grass seeds and those which are deep and high-sided are for carrying water. The larger ones are good for carrying food as well as babies, and the smaller versions are useful tools for scraping and digging earth to find food.

Coolamons are painted for ceremonial purposes. These are made from wood, although other found objects (like hubcaps or cooking pot lids) are also used.

The many uses of grinding stones

Grinding stones are made up of two stones: a flat base slab or a bowl cut into the rock, as well as a rounded handheld smaller stone, the hammerstone. The user applies pressure with the hammerstone to grind, crush or pound the material.

Grinding stones are used to prepare food for cooking. Aboriginal people ground all types of vegetables and grains into flour or paste to bake at the campfire. In the dry desert regions on Country, they were particularly useful tools for making bread from grass seeds, as not much else grew there.

These stones were also used to pound up meat, in the production of medicines, and to grind ochres for ceremonial painting.

Paul says

Because grinding stones are so heavy, most people left them on Country for when they could get back there later. Grinding stones have been found in many Australian deserts (for example, the Simpson Desert) in now-abandoned campsites.

Desert people were very respectful of each other and did not take someone else's property if they found it. But the same can't be said for many of the colonists who came through later.

The many uses of fire

Cooking fires and slow ovens are essential kitchen tools on Country. Cooking fires might be designed to produce hot ash-free coals to roast meat dropped on the top, or to produce warm ashes in which seed cakes or insects can be lightly singed, or as hot ash fires in which fish are cooked whole in their skins. Fire also provides light, warmth and security. Its smoke wards off troublesome insects like mosquitoes and bush flies.

Fire is also used in firestick farming. Small grass fires were often deliberately lit to make animals run from grass cover so that they were easier to catch and corner, and to prevent big bushfires. Such fires were also burnt before rains to ensure fresh shoots came up which would attract animals to munch on them.

Aboriginal people have even invented ways of carrying fire in a wooden holder, so they don't have to go to all that effort to rekindle it each time. And, yes, there are many Fire Dreamings across the continent.

In Alyawarr and Arrernte Countries, it's believed travelling bushfires gave 'skins' or classes to animals, plants and areas of Country, in order to classify the environment for connection to certain people with the same skins.

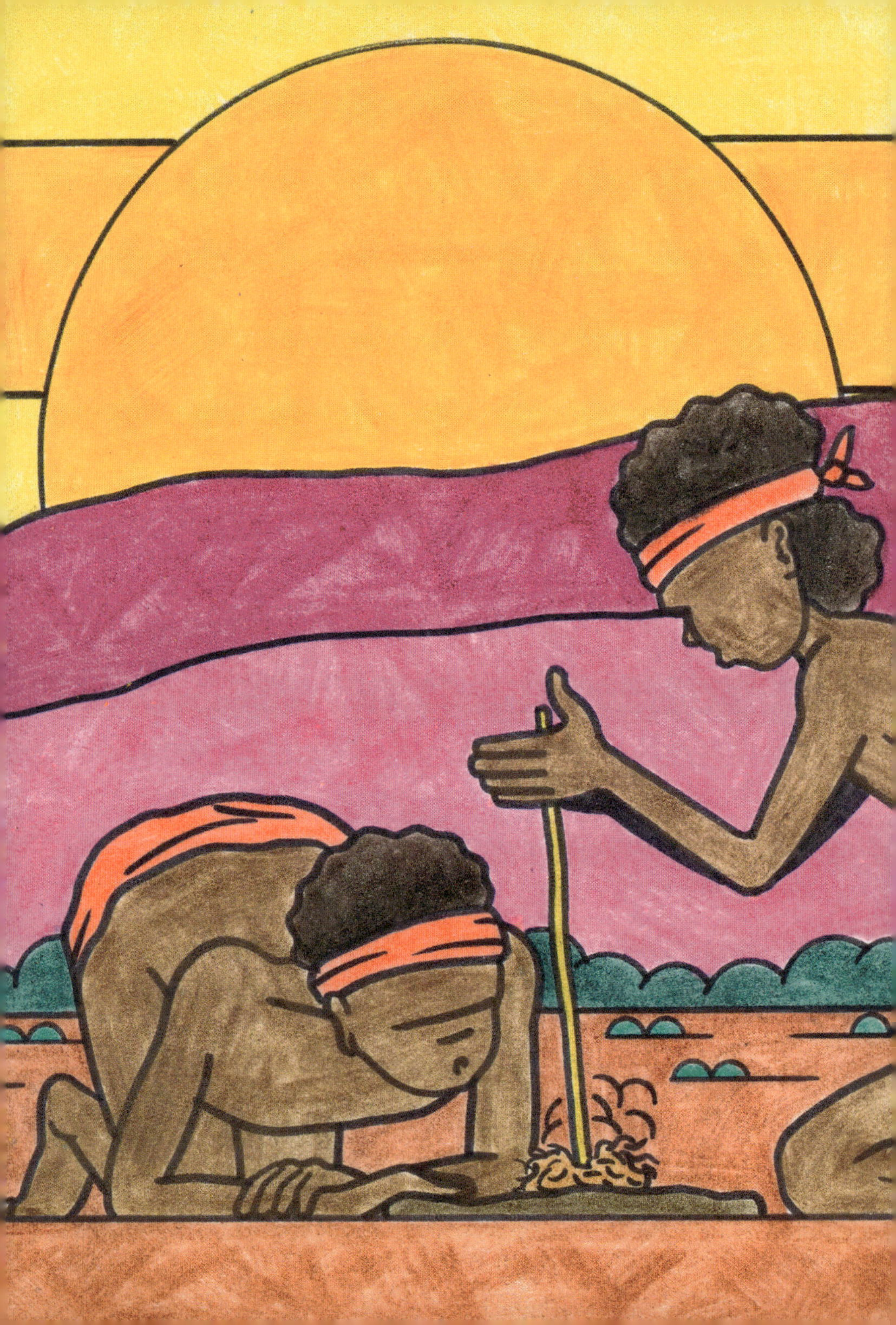

How to make a fire

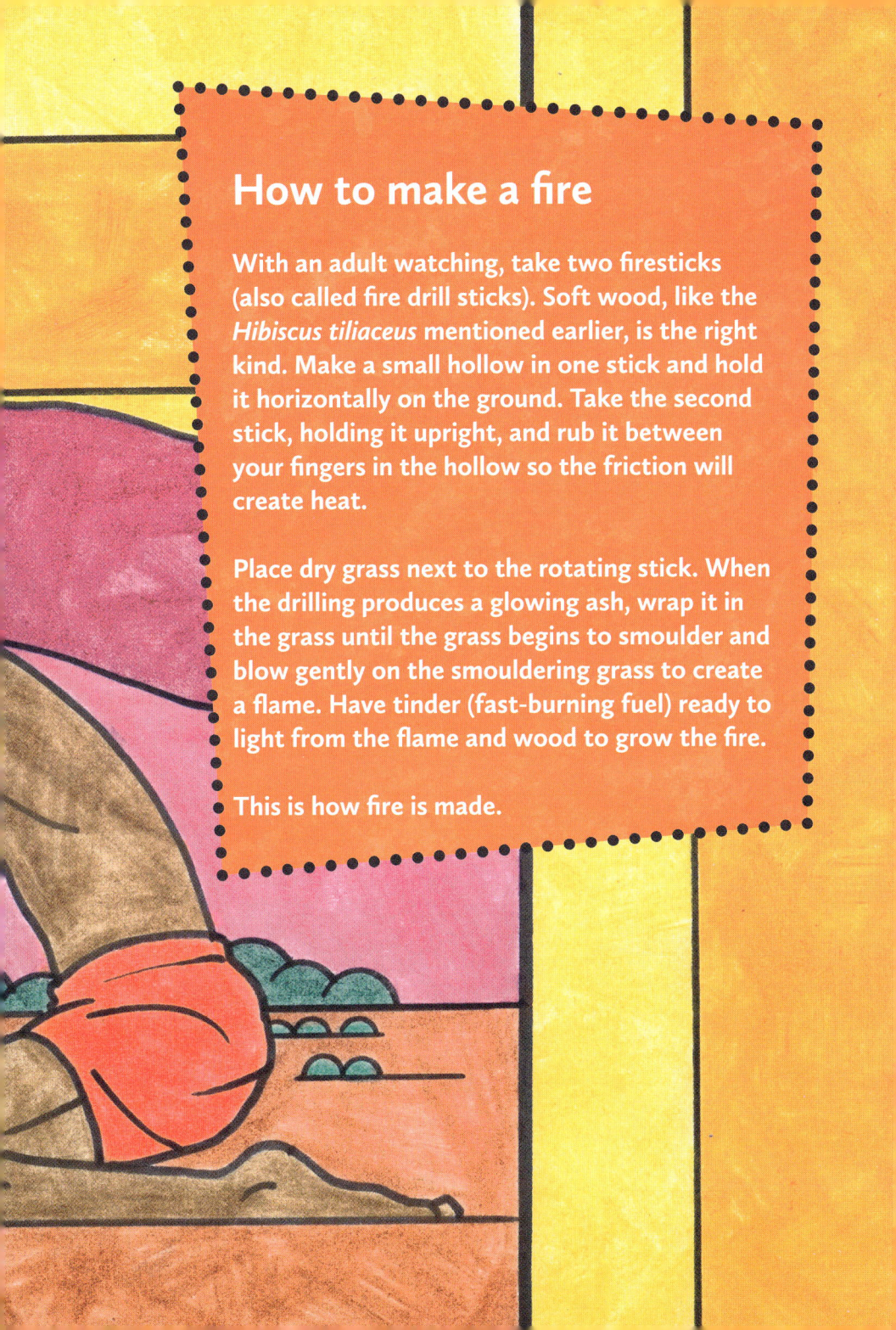

With an adult watching, take two firesticks (also called fire drill sticks). Soft wood, like the *Hibiscus tiliaceus* mentioned earlier, is the right kind. Make a small hollow in one stick and hold it horizontally on the ground. Take the second stick, holding it upright, and rub it between your fingers in the hollow so the friction will create heat.

Place dry grass next to the rotating stick. When the drilling produces a glowing ash, wrap it in the grass until the grass begins to smoulder and blow gently on the smouldering grass to create a flame. Have tinder (fast-burning fuel) ready to light from the flame and wood to grow the fire.

This is how fire is made.

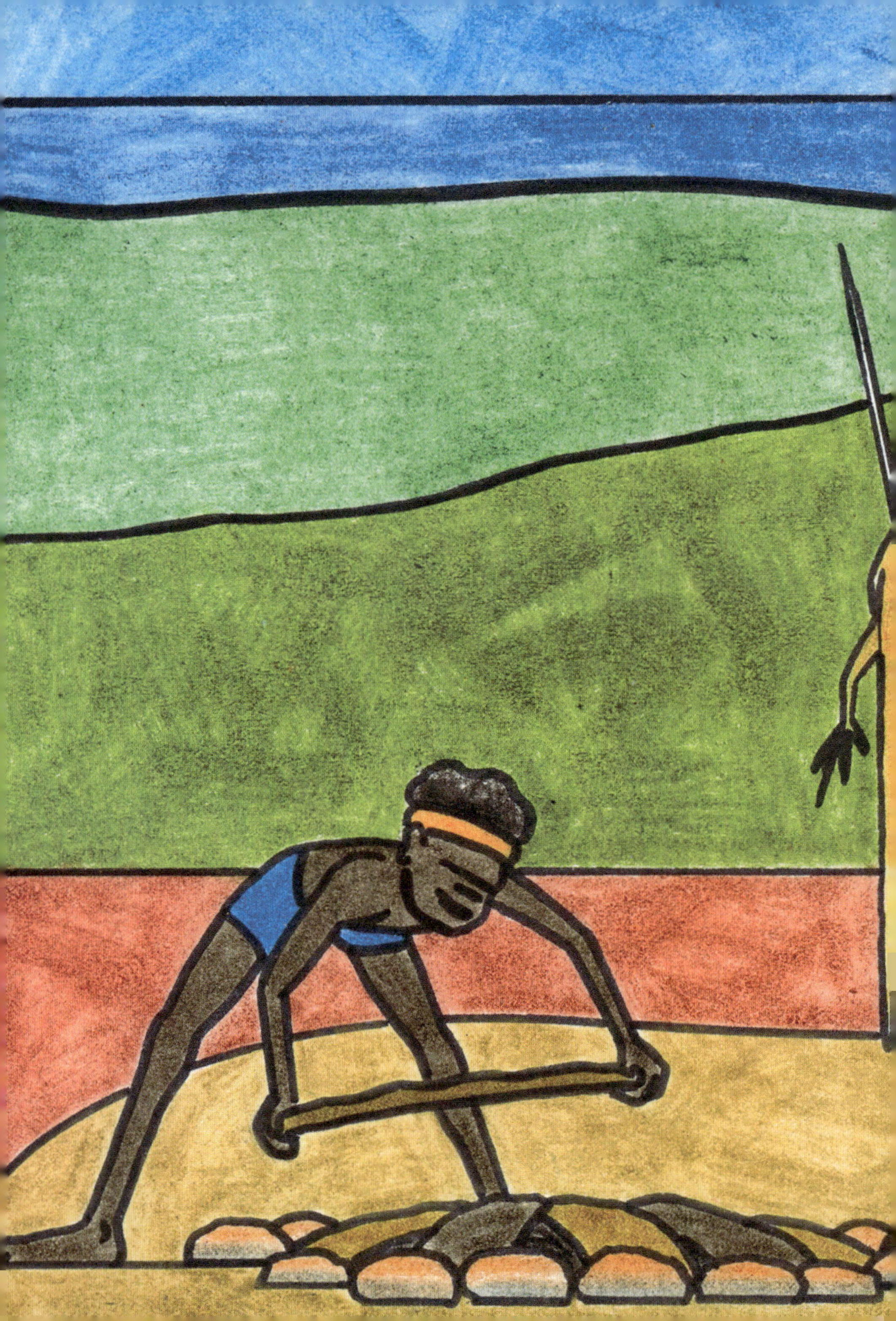

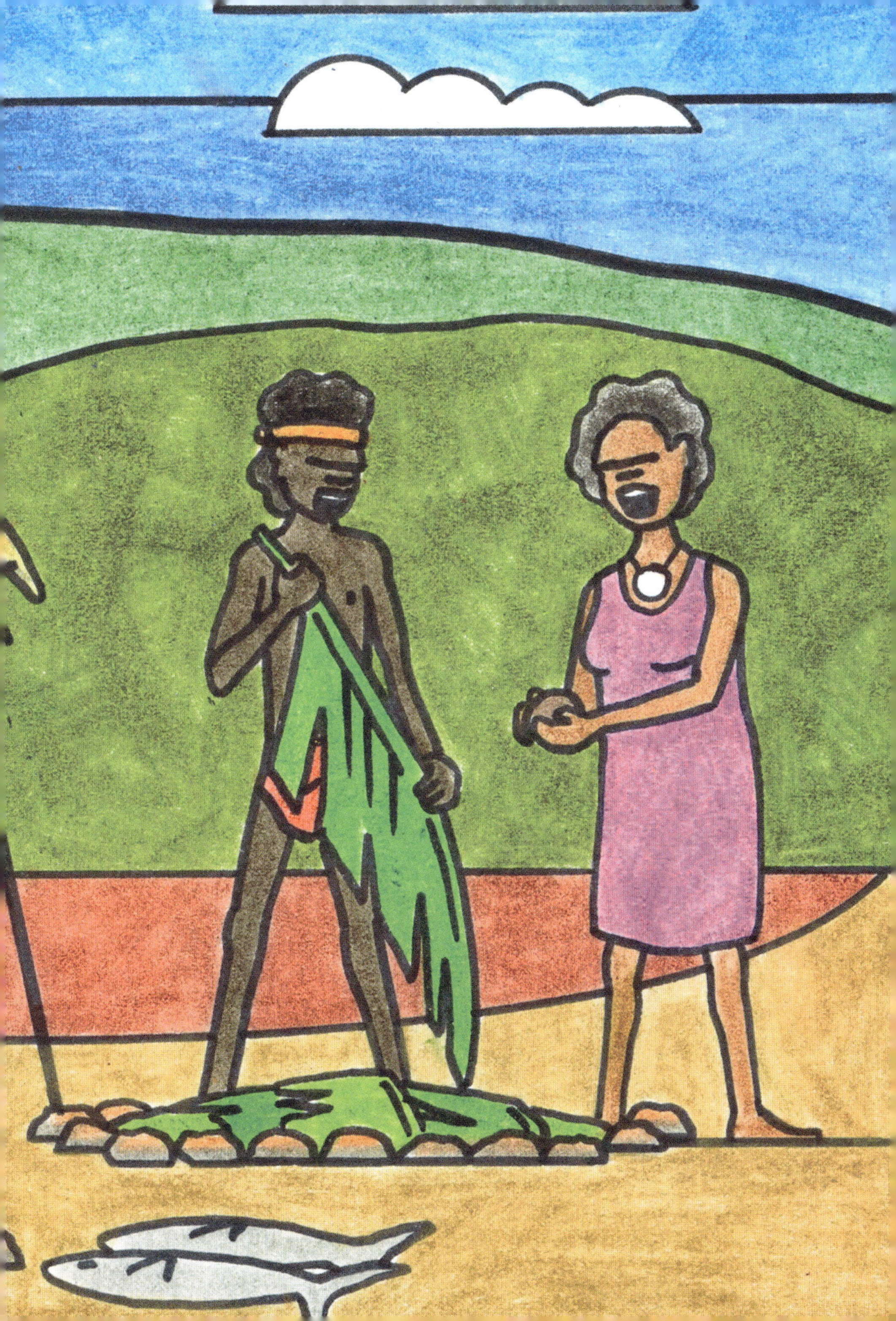

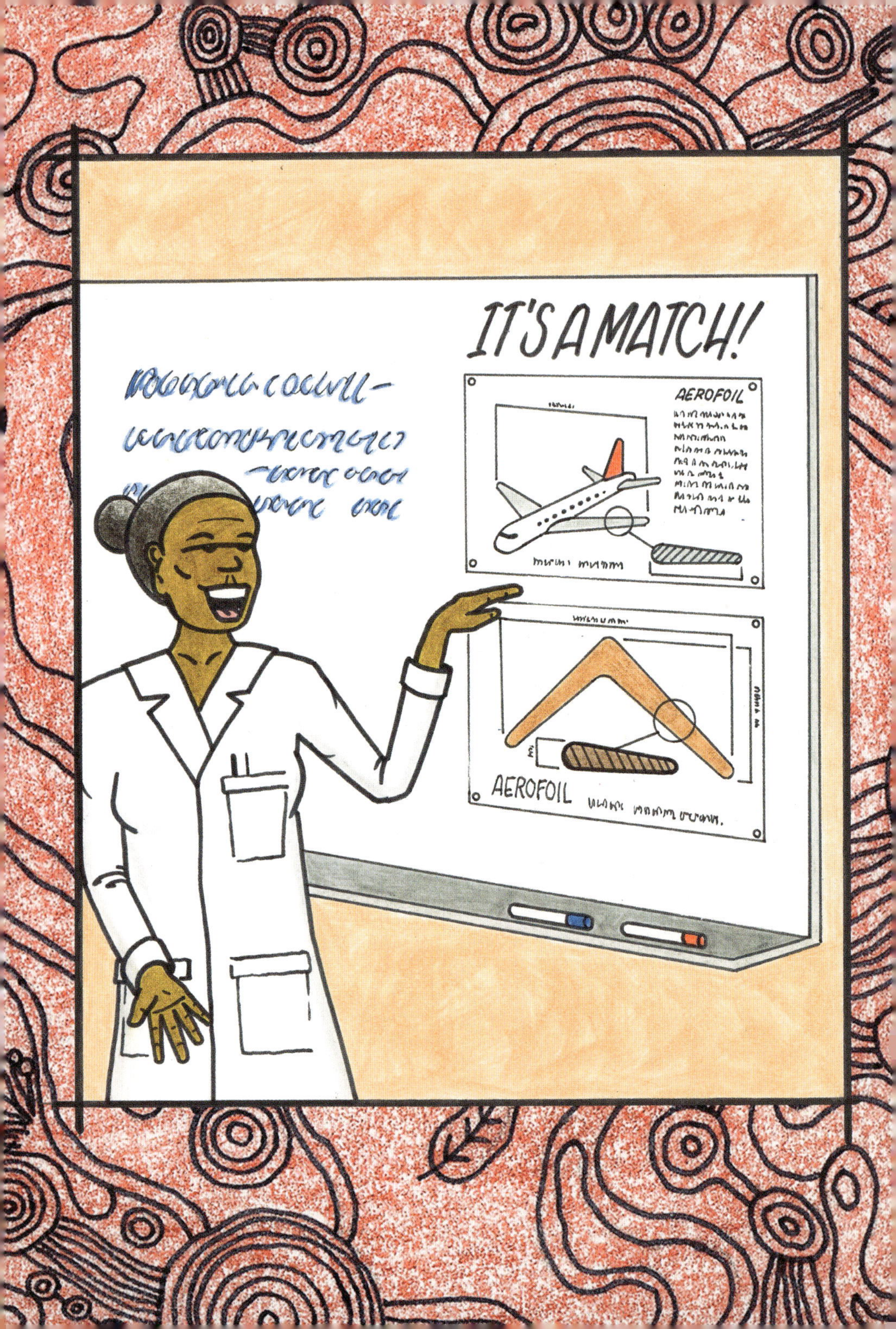
IT'S A MATCH!
AEROFOIL
AEROFOIL

Chapter 5:
The first engineers on Country

One of the most astounding Aboriginal inventions is the returning boomerang. Did you know that it is also the world's earliest aerofoil? An aerofoil is a surface that helps to lift or control an aircraft or sailing boat by making use of the currents of air through which it moves. An aerofoil is a secret weapon for controlling flight and motion.

Both wings of a returning boomerang have an aerofoil-shaped cross-section just like an aircraft wing. The boomerang is flat on one side and curved on the other with one edge thicker, which helps it stay in the air due to lift. Lift happens when the air flowing up and over the curved side of the wing has further to travel than the air flowing past the flat side. The air moving over the curved surface has to travel more quickly in order to reach the other edge of the wing.

A boomerang is also a very special type of aerofoil because it spins from the centre as it flies, so the amount of lift changes across its flying surface. The two sides of a boomerang are of different lengths and have different air speeds flowing over them. So as the boomerang spins, the force of the air is uneven. This causes the section of the boomerang moving in the same direction that the boomerang is going to move that bit faster than the section going in the opposite direction.

But after a while, it can't cope with those opposing forces, so it starts to turn in and follow a circular route back to the thrower. It's like it changes its mind, or just gets tired, and wants to return home!

Restructuring the landscape

In the times before British colonisation of Australia, the land was full of designed structures that Aboriginal people made. These changes made to the landscape weren't as obvious as the intensive building and farming practices of the newcomers, who brought many of their own animals and plants, tools and equipment, with little understanding of the advanced systems of landcare that Aboriginal people knew about.

The Aboriginal system of landcare and land use for farming plants and animals was based on the laws of science and kinship and included advanced netting practices and the skilful use of existing land features and seasonal rainfall patterns. The landcare system was set up to ensure that species could regenerate and remain healthy.

Aboriginal people made interventions in the landscape that would be barely noticeable if you weren't looking for them, most of them not intended to be permanent. But some of the most remarkable of these engineered structures are still there today, like the famous rock-wall eel traps located in the traditional Country of the Gunditjmara people in south-eastern Australia that have been given UNESCO World Heritage status!

The Brewarrina fish traps

In this drawing, you can see the fish traps (ngunnhu) in the Barwon River at Brewarrina, close to the tribal lands of the Wangaaybuyan, Wailwan, Kamilaroi/Gamilaraay and Muruwari peoples. Their sacred history tells how the Ancestral Being Baiame cast his fishing net over the river, which gave his two sons the idea to design the traps in this layout. Baiame gave different clans and family groups a rock wall each to maintain and fish from. All the traps had different names and Spirit Ancestors that guarded the fisheries from strangers. If anyone crossed the Kirragurra Rock that was not part of the family, the Ancestral Being might visit upon them sickness or other misfortunes, so people knew to stay away!

Schools of fish travelled upstream to spawn (breed) at particular times of year. After large schools of fish had passed through, the gates in the walls could be closed after them by blocking them with rocks. Once the fish reached the larger pools, the hunters would hit the water to scare them into the smaller, more enclosed pools where they were easier to spear and catch. The traps in the middle of the river could be used when the river was slow and low in water, and the ones higher up the banks were for use when the river flooded.

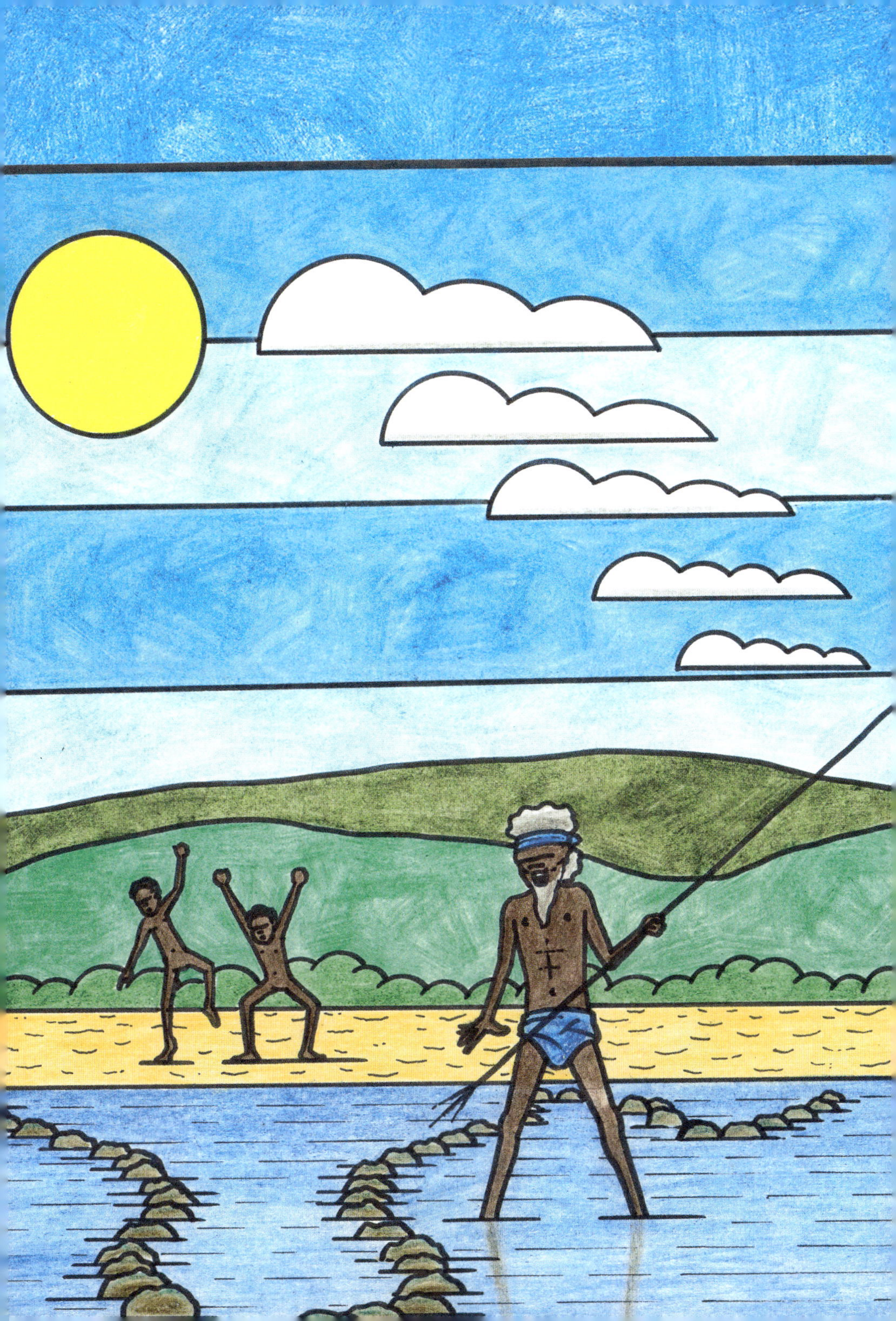

Netting and trapping practices

The Georgina River basin in central-west Queensland is dry for most of the year, but each wet season the rivers fill and flow towards Lake Eyre. Then as the dry season starts, the flow of water slows, leaving large, full waterholes. Fishing teams handled nets as large as 15–24 metres in length, standing in water up to their waists to catch whole schools of yellowbelly or bream that were trapped. As the water went down further, smaller groups of fish, yabbies and abundant water lilies could be collected.

These large nets, often painted with bands of red and yellow ochre, were also used on land to trap ground animals, in particular kangaroos and emus with nets that were up to 30–40 metres in length. Made of rope similar to the fibres used by the Lardil to make dugong nets, they were stretched across pathways made between foliage walls to construct V-shaped laneways that led to waterholes. There was no way out if an unsuspecting emu or kangaroo made their way down there. It would be speared near the narrow end of the V.

What are those rock walls for?

The British explorers who first came to the Wellesley Islands in the early 1880s were impressed by the rock-wall fish traps they saw there lining the seashores, although it took some time for them to work out what they were. In the low tide, they looked like 'walled-in paddocks of some length'. But it was only when the tides came in and filled them up with water that they realised these were fish traps.

How do rock-walled fish traps work?

Rock-wall traps take many shapes, but they are usually built in rough semicircles up to a height of one metre with the trap ends pointing towards the land side, and they become naturally cemented in place by oysters. When the tide comes in the water goes over the wall and the fish come in towards the shore. When the tide goes out, and the water drops below the top of the wall, the fish are trapped, and easy to spear or grab in a net.

Rock-wall traps were made in many different parts of the Australian continent on inland waterways, coastal mudflats and rock platforms. They have been used in freshwater rivers and streams as well as marine habitats in the sea and ocean. People used them differently in different parts of freshwater and saltwater Countries. And that means there were different types of foods collected, mostly fish and eels. But in the Wellesley Islands, which have the largest number of these fish traps than anywhere else in Australia, turtles were also trapped and mud crabs could be found living in holes in the walls, not to mention the constant supply of oysters growing on the stones.

To build a fish trap required more than basic knowledge of how to build a wall. Making and using a rock-wall trap is not as easy as it looks. Aboriginal people had to know all about the tidal flows at high tide and low tide at different times of year and be prepared for storm surges. People also had to know all there is to know about the lifestyle and habits of their favourite seafood, such as when it's their breeding season, and when to expect the big schools of fish to swim by. And, as we know, the seashore is always changing, especially when a tsunami or cyclone strikes.

What the Barkandji people did on land and water

The Barkandji people of the Barka or Darling River region made wickerwork and rock-wall dams for catching fish. They used tree branches to direct the movement of land animals into nets and holes in the ground. They also covered streams with large nets to catch flocks of birds. And, in the dry season, they protected the water supply with a timber or bark covering so that it wouldn't evaporate. That's like storing the water in a container.

Paul says

In the Wellesley Islands in the Gulf of Carpentaria, the tidal conditions can get complicated. Most days there is only one tide, but on some days of the lunar month there are two tides. During the double tides there is not much movement, but at 'springs' (twice in a lunar month) the tides are much higher than normal. And in the wet season the tidal flows are even more extreme, like the weather, with huge quantities of water flowing downriver into the gulf as well as storm surges during cyclones.

To deal with these different levels of water, the Kaiadilt people in the South Wellesley Islands built several walls of traps (ngurruwarra) up the beachfront and into the sea, so at least one trap could do its job no matter how high or low the tide might be at the time. When a turtle or dugong (sea cow) was caught, they used a specially designed barbed spearhead to keep a grip on their prize catch. They believed that the original design of the trap was dreamed up by their Ancestors, Bujuku (Black Crane) and Kaarku (Seagull).

If the tides didn't suit the location of the traps, the Lardil people of the North Wellesley Islands were more likely to take things into their own hands, using large nets and groups of hunters to catch not just one but several dugong in one go. They placed dugong nets in muddy waters, with one group of men holding the poles connected to the large nets ready to close them, and another group on rafts herding the dugong into the traps, while yet another was on standby to assist in drowning them by holding their tails up and their noses down in the water.

Advances in Aboriginal fibre technologies

Rock technology was only one type of Aboriginal technology used. Fibre was another. Though research in this area is still in its early days, architects, anthropologists and now biochemical engineers are thinking through many of the traditional First Nations' knowledges to find new ways of using traditional material culture to replace plastic and other non-renewable materials with more sustainable and biodegradable plant-fibre products. Such products can combine strength with flexibility, just like the nets and trap designs that you have been reading about.

Many grasses, vegetable fibres, plant stems, vines, canes, reeds and bamboos combined with traditional fibrecraft like knotting, weaving, plaiting, thatching, binding, netmaking and basketry, were used to manufacture traditional artefacts. First Nations peoples in Australia and other parts of the world have renewed interest in the potential for these technologies to provide alternative materials for product design and even building construction.

We already know of one Aboriginal man, Colin Saltmere Pwerle from the Indjalandji-Dhidhanu mob, who has set up a company to make a range of new products by adding spinifex fibres to them to provide strength: cement, paper, latex and medical gels. The use of spinifex resin and fibre in the construction of insulation materials for the roofs and walls of buildings is also an exciting new product that we'll see more of and you will read about in chapter 7. These new ways of investing in Indigenous material culture and manufacturing technologies are an exciting new adventure for us all.

89

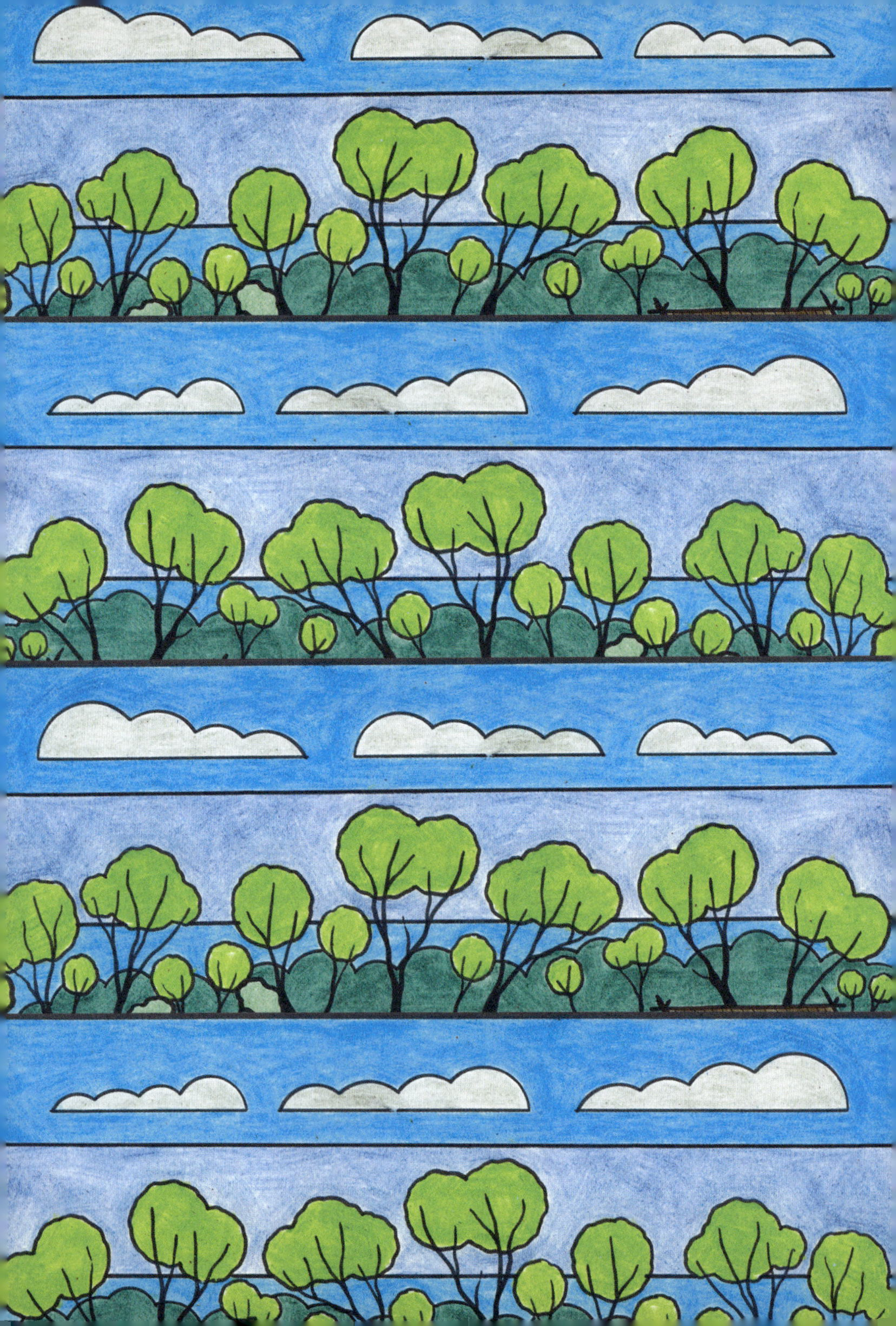

Chapter 6:
Setting up a camp

Before colonisation, Aboriginal people moved around their 'land estates' or, on the coast, their 'sea estates'. The range of travel for open or free hunting and collecting was restricted by the borders of your territory or Country as well as obligations to the Dreamings related to particular sites.

At any one time, different groups of people would be at different sites on Country, hunting, gathering and (except in desert regions) fishing. Aboriginal people knew (and many still know) their place in the world and were familiar with its unique geography and histories of place.

These small local groups set up camps for a single day or up to several weeks. And, throughout the continent that we now call Australia, there were bigger gatherings of many tribes and language groups, also known as 'Nations', when many peoples from different Countries came together, sometimes for weeks at a time or even longer.

In good seasons, when there was enough food and enough fresh, clean water to support a hundred or more people who might come together, there was feasting, celebrations, ceremonies, initiations, the arrangement of marriages and dispute and conflict resolution, as well as time for healing and reconciliation.

The rules of how to accommodate all those people were particularly complicated at these times.

Setting up a campsite

A particular campsite might be chosen because of its natural qualities of surface, vegetation and proximity to trees for shade, a waterhole or a river. Hunting grounds and engineered spaces, like you read about in the last chapter, were also important, as was the connection to the right animals and plants and known sacred sites.

Campsites could be distributed over large estates, just as the number of people living in a camp at any one time could vary from one family up to several hundred people. That's enough people to fill a small town or suburb!

And just like the way people live today, there were separate places and shelters for during the day and for night when everyone went back to their family group. If you were older or didn't have a family, you lived with other adults or young people. The single men would sleep together in one shelter and the single women in another. Some people weren't allowed to mix with others. There were rules about where you could or could not go. This was to respect people's privacy, and to protect people from conflicts and differences between kinship and skin groups.

During the day, people were very busy, but at night and in the early evening people came together to talk, cook and eat their meals. People felt safe in their communities and late into the night could hear each other talking and singing across the campsite. Sometimes they all joined in together!

The camp layout was not random but highly organised, and a similar plan was used when people moved on to the next campsite, so that people always knew where they were in relationship to other people and felt safe.

Basic types of shelter

Shelter was often minimal in the hot desert or grasslands where building material was not available in large quantities, and most people liked to sleep out in the open. Some people reused structures that had been made previously.

The most useful bush furniture was a simple windbreak that could be quickly made up using various types of grass or foliage.

In different regions across the continent, there were many different types of temporary or more permanent structures. In the next chapter, we will discuss in more detail the types of shelters and more permanent housing that Aboriginal people built in different parts of the continent.

How to build a windbreak

Windbreaks were the most useful outdoor furniture, and they doubled up as dividers between groups and spaces. They could be built just high enough for people to peep over them and to provide protection from cold wind.

Windbreaks were traditionally made from grass, sticks, vines, and foliage from bushes and trees, all woven together.

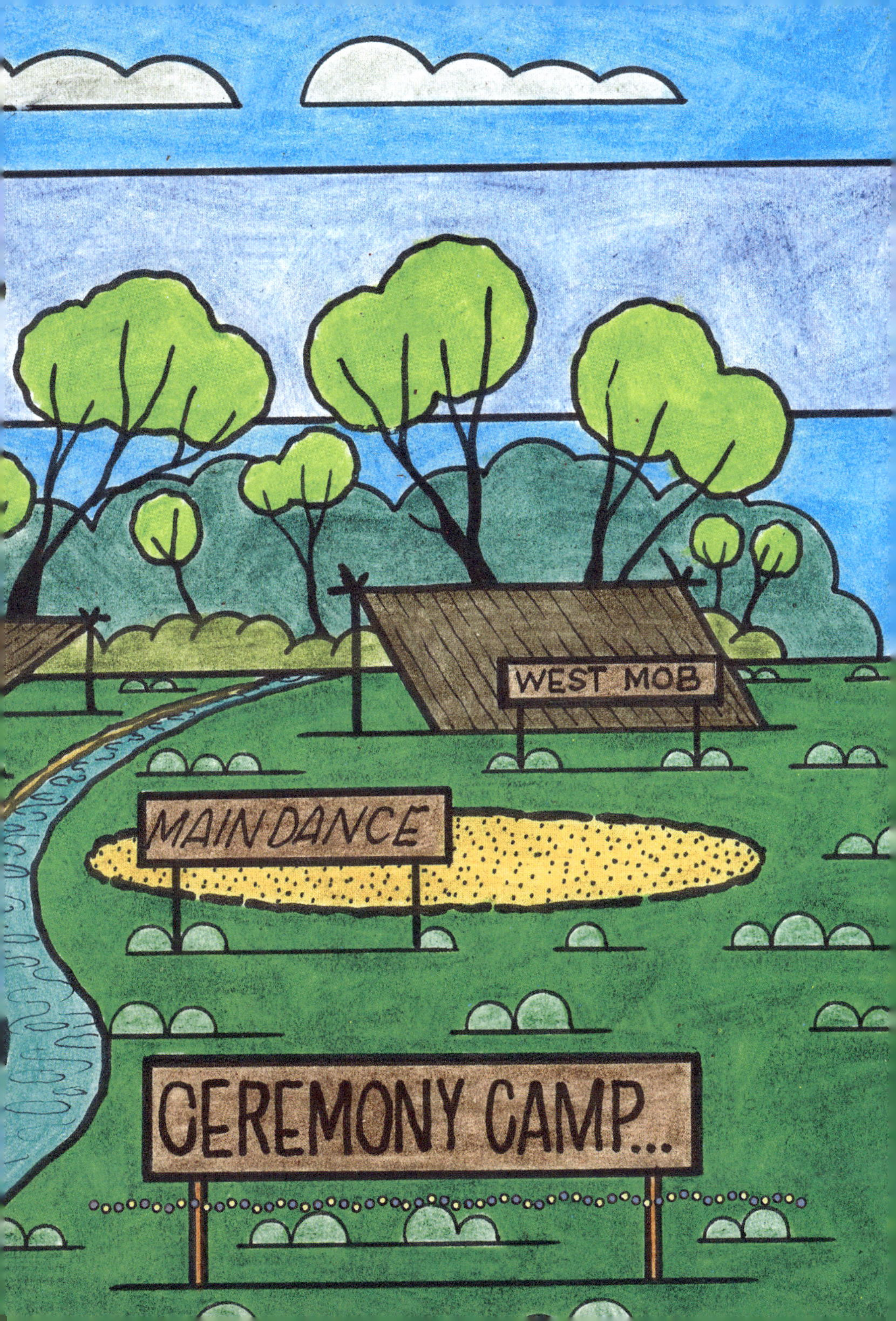
WEST MOB
MAIN DANCE
CEREMONY CAMP...

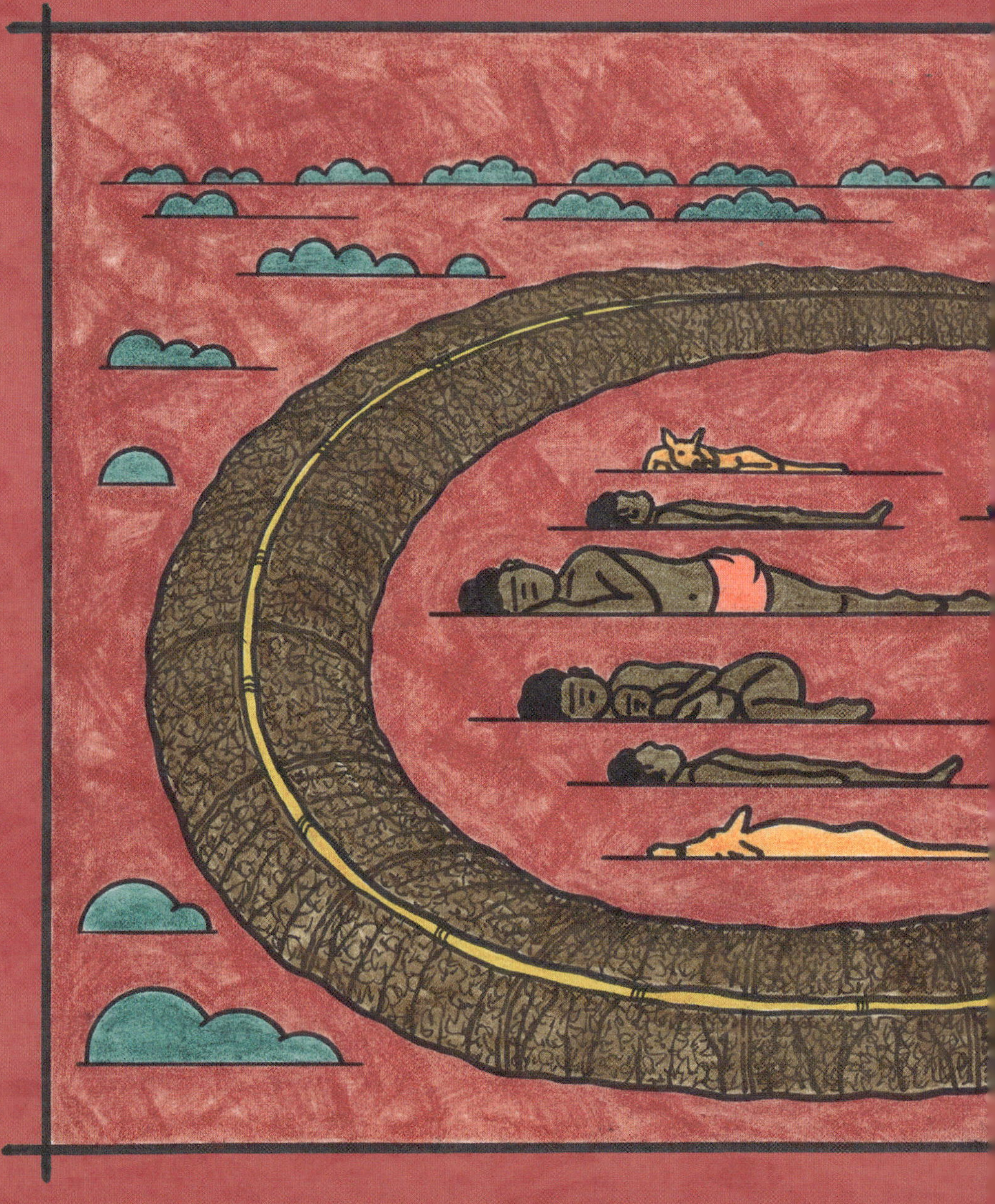

Summer nights on Country

On warm, dry nights, people slept under the stars, whom they knew very well and could talk to, studying their behaviour and their journey across the sky, sometimes singing the sacred songs about their Dreamings, such as the Seven Sisters (Pleiades), Venus, the Morning Star or the Southern Cross.

People slept in their groups around a shared fire for warmth and protection, at times sheltered by windbreaks. The smoke was a repellent for mosquitoes and other biting insects and animals. The fires were placed beside each person or family group.

Here is a typical map of a camp, showing the sleeping arrangements and where the windbreak was placed.

97

Paul says

A temporary traveller's camp

I once went with some Lardil men to catch dugong near Sydney Island for a couple of days. On the way, we set up a traveller's camp for one night and I got some useful lessons in the Old People's ways from an Elder, Fred Jaurth, whose surname was adapted from the name of one of his totems, bluefish (Jarrarr).

There was myself and some other younger and older Lardil men as well. Fred was in charge, directing us all to work, and we followed his instructions about how to set up a short-stay campsite. This is how it went:

Two men went up the beach with their three-pronged spears (kurrumbu). One man headed to the open country behind the beach and chopped down a dozen bloodwood saplings, to make 1-metre-high stakes, which he then planted in a circle about 5 metres in diameter. I had the job of getting the firewood. Meanwhile, two other men found a big haul of beach vine (thaburra) that they separated and draped over the wooden stakes to make a windbreak (wungkurr).

As they were finishing, the fishermen came back with several large fish they had speared and a bucket of mud crabs. By early evening, we were sitting by the campfire, with fish and crabs roasting in the coals, and a pile of native oak tree leaves (wunhan) ready to use as plates.

After dinner, Fred got very talkative about his Mirndiyan (Lardil for Dreaming). He wasn't just talking to us, he was talking directly to his Country. Later that night I was woken by him singing in his sleep. He told me later that he was receiving a gift of knowledge from the ancestral spirits: the warrior Warrenbi and the Wallaby Woman, Maguraa, who Warrenbi was in love with. This is the way Lardil people get new songs and dances, through gifts in dreams from the spirit people in their Country.

When we left, the foliage from the wungkurr was removed. The wooden posts would have stood up for a while and the site was most likely revisited by any or all of the men at different times. It was one of probably fifty or more such campsites being maintained on the Mornington Island coastline. Our camp was at an old base camp called Kenthawu that had been there for centuries, well before Old Fred and his family were taken to the Mornington Island mission when he was a young boy.

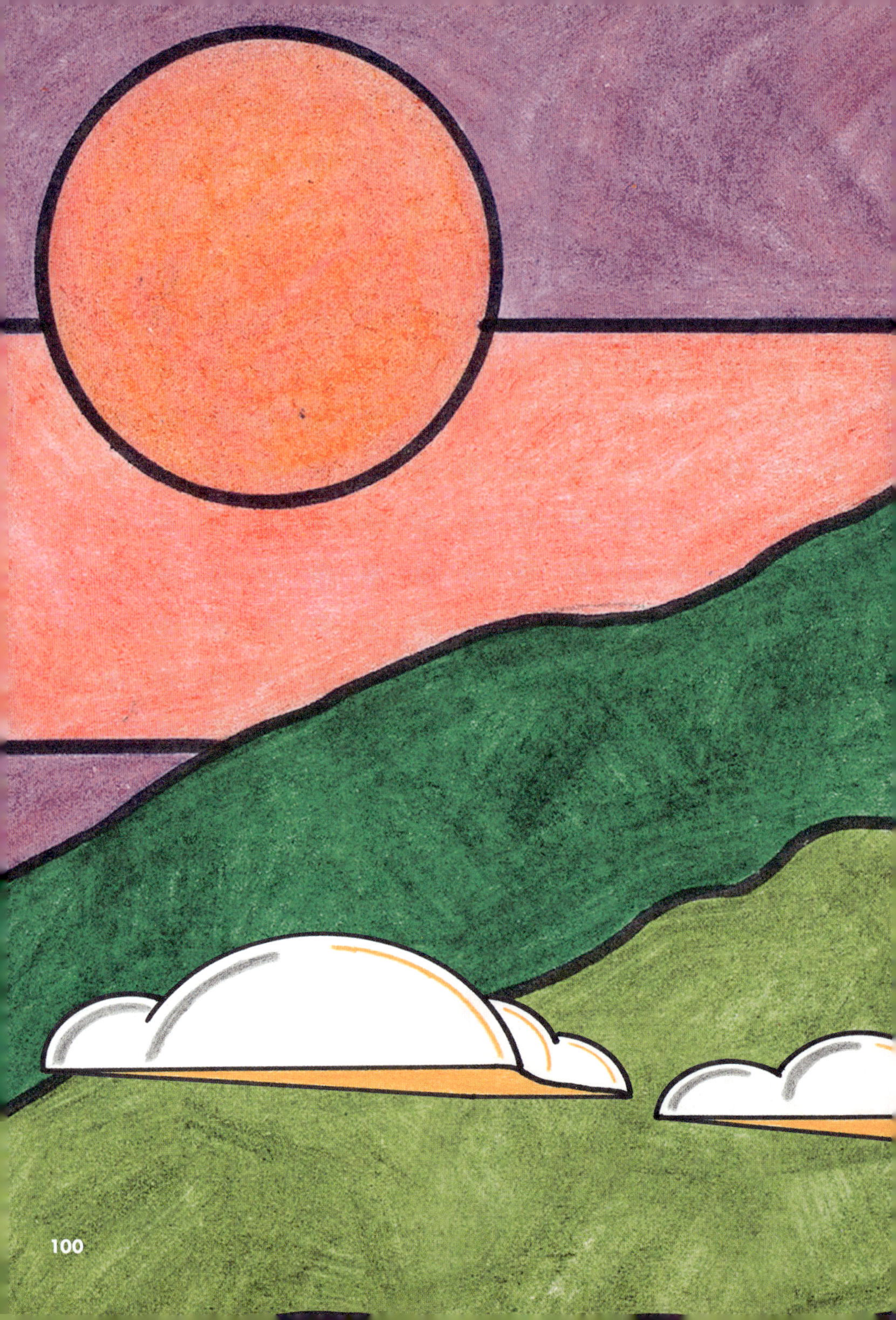

Alison says

Finding your place on Country

Life on Country was an inclusive relationship to your homelands and your community and everything in it, including your next of kin in the animal and plant as well as the non-human worlds. As you moved about your Country it demanded things of you to ensure the health of all those relationships and your place in it.

You had to learn a lot, respect your Elders, deal with difficult people and changes happening all around you. There was always the possibility of conflict. Perhaps someone stole something or there were shortages. There were births, deaths and marriages. Some people had to move on, or new people joined the camp.

And always there was Country itself, like a difficult if much-loved person with a big personality that was expressed through the weather and the seasons and everything that happened there. Country was also the mother. She was the nurturer, full of great kindnesses. She was the place that people returned to again and again throughout their lives. And the care for her was the most important thing. This is still important today.

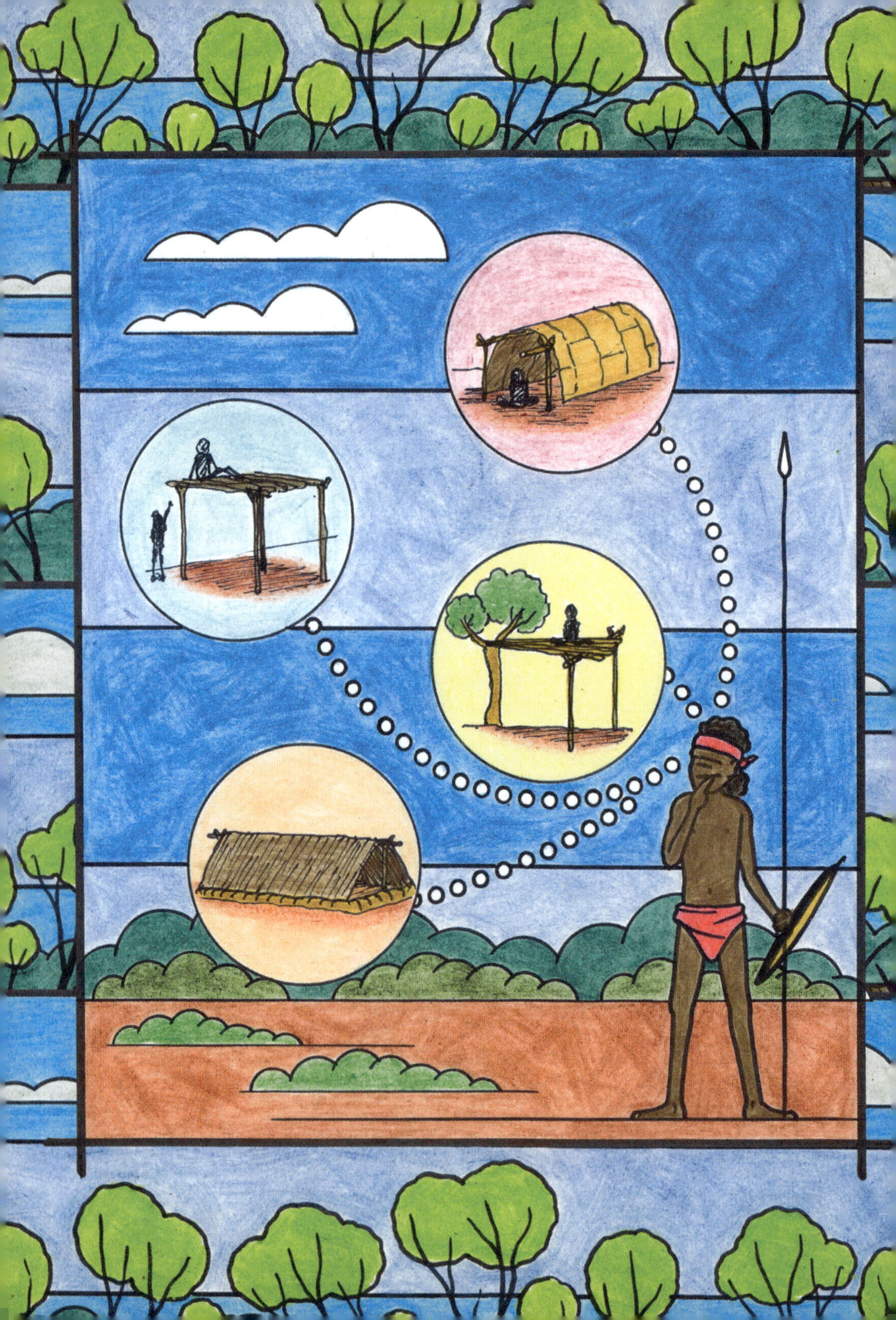

Chapter 7:
Building a shelter

Most Aboriginal language groups had a range of different types of buildings and shelters that they knew how to build on their type of Country. The way they were made depended on the weather and the climate, how long you planned to stay and the available materials.

These building materials might include tree limbs, bark sheets, grasses, leaves, vines, stones, clay and mud. In the colder, southern regions of Australia, people built more solid closed spaces, with stone and bark and wooden walls, as well as grass-thatched, domed structures mixed with clay and soil to keep in the warmth.

Across coastal and particularly tropical northern areas, Aboriginal builders were experts in weaving and plaiting grasses, pandanus and coconut palm leaves to make many different types of structures. Beach vine and handmade rope or twine was used to fix the sections together. Bendable vines and saplings made these buildings good at standing up to wild tropical storms. Tropical housing also included raised ledges and platforms to cope with storm water surges, flooding and muddy surrounds.

In open campsites and shelters in drier parts of the country, floor spaces could also be dug and excavated, with pits and trenches for drainage and storing things. And sometimes shelters with high platforms were built to sleep above the dust, biting insects and snakes and to store food and other precious things so dogs and other animals couldn't get to them.

Demountable buildings and flatpacks

When people decided to move on, when they had used up the local food supply, or when the ceremonies were over, they often left the structures there to use next time. At the least, they left the frames and posts fixed firmly in the ground. The poles and posts were made using the strongest types of timber available so they could last for a long time. The bark roofs and walls could be removed and laid flat on the ground so they wouldn't warp or blow away. The bark sheets were weighted down with logs or grindstones and other heavy tools and equipment that you couldn't take with you. Then everything was waiting for you when you got back.

A shelter could be rebuilt within minutes upon a return visit to a campsite. So easy, like an IKEA flatpack, only better quality and made of more sustainable materials!

Buildings for cold and wet weather

Sleeping out in the open was not always an option on Country. In the tropical rainforests of (mainly) north-eastern Australia where there is frequent rain, clusters of connected domes were made from woven (latticed) cane or sapling frames clad with bark, layers of thatched grass or palm leaves.

Similarly, on the cold, wet, south-western coast of Tasmania, winter domes were grass-thatched, and lined with paperbark inside. And in western Victoria, people built earth-clad dome-shaped buildings often fitted with a porch and a vent to let out the smoke from the inside fire.

Also in western Victoria, low circular stone-walled buildings were constructed. While many were windbreaks, some had timber-frame roofs that were made strong enough for an adult to stand on the roof and fix it when necessary to keep it weatherproof.

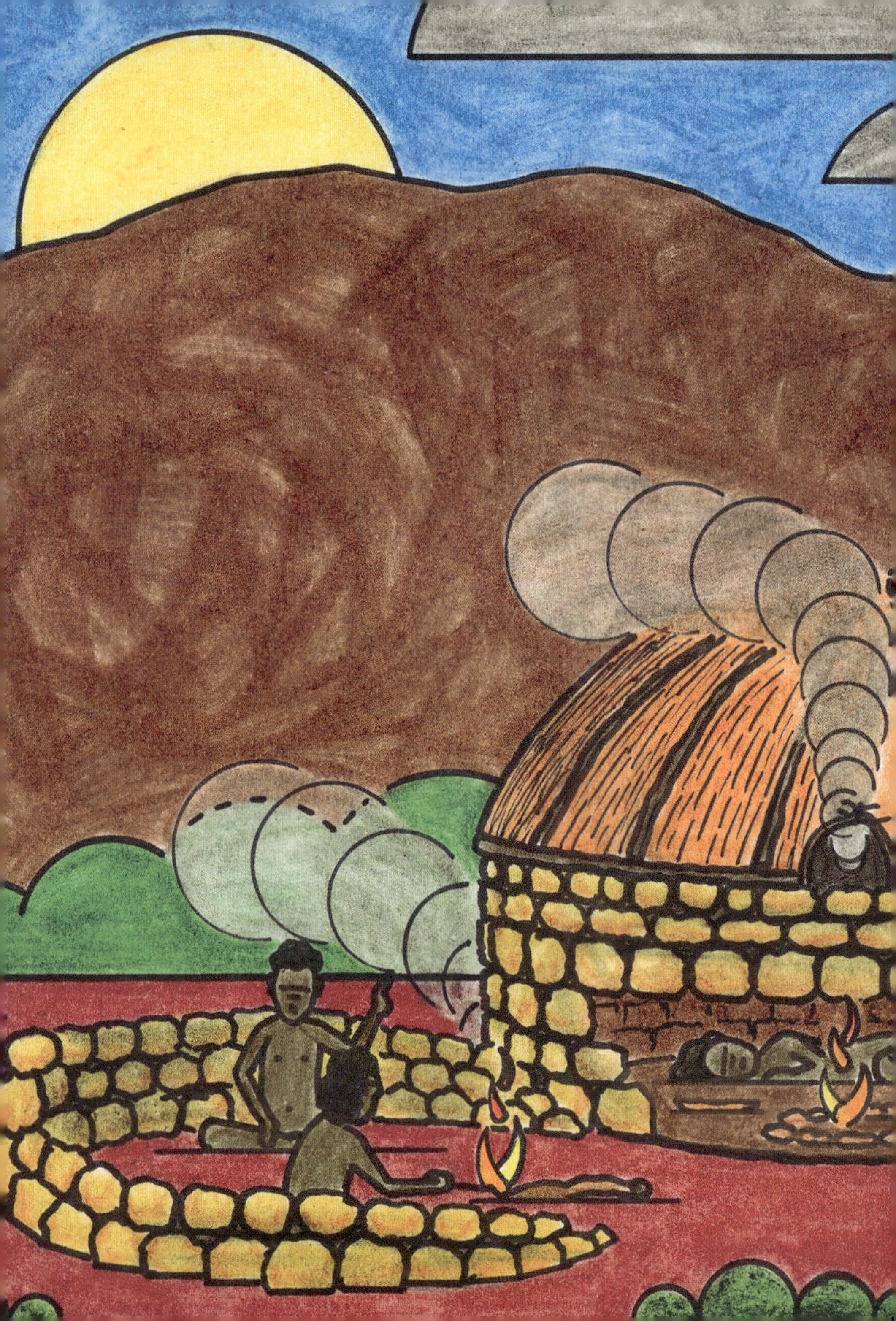

Spinifex grass walls and roofs

You already read about the miracle fibre technology created from spinifex in chapter 5. Traditional Aboriginal people from Central Australia were already making roofs and walls with compressed spinifex grass before contemporary architects and construction engineers took an interest. They are now experimenting with using this material to make new modern products today following their earlier example. One way is that the nano-fibres are used to strengthen recycled paper and make medical gels, as they're biodegradable.

Alison says

What the British colonists didn't know

What the British thought about the way Aboriginal people lived was wrong in many, many ways. All they could compare the lifestyle of Aboriginal people with was their own British colonial farms, cottages, big houses, villages, towns and castles – a life that was static and walled in permanently. They couldn't see that the mobile life was the good life, and spending one day here, a few days, weeks or months there, was much kinder to Country and kinder to the people. It allowed everyone to live as part of the natural cycles of Country so that everyone could learn about their Country, look after their Country, give back to Country, work with Country, and take from Country just a bit at a time.

The British didn't think the kinds of structures that Aboriginal and Torres Strait Islander peoples built were even proper shelters, camps or houses, and they didn't know that the way the First Peoples managed their big Country estates was a type of farming that was better suited to these lands.

They didn't get to sleep under the stars, full in the knowledge of their place in the world like the Aboriginal people did. Even Captain Cook wrote in his diary in 1770 that they were the happiest people he had ever witnessed because the land and sea provided everything they would ever need.

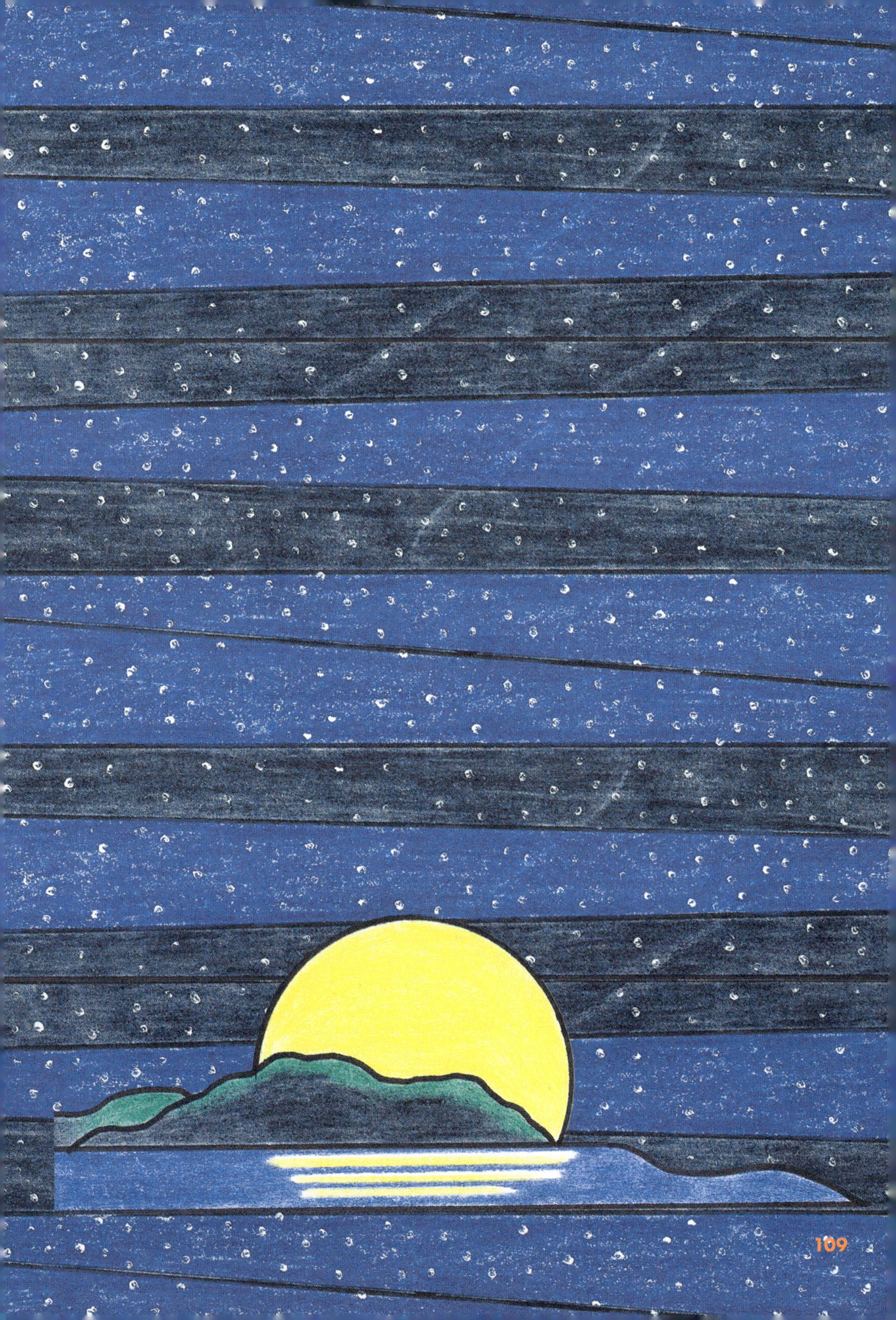

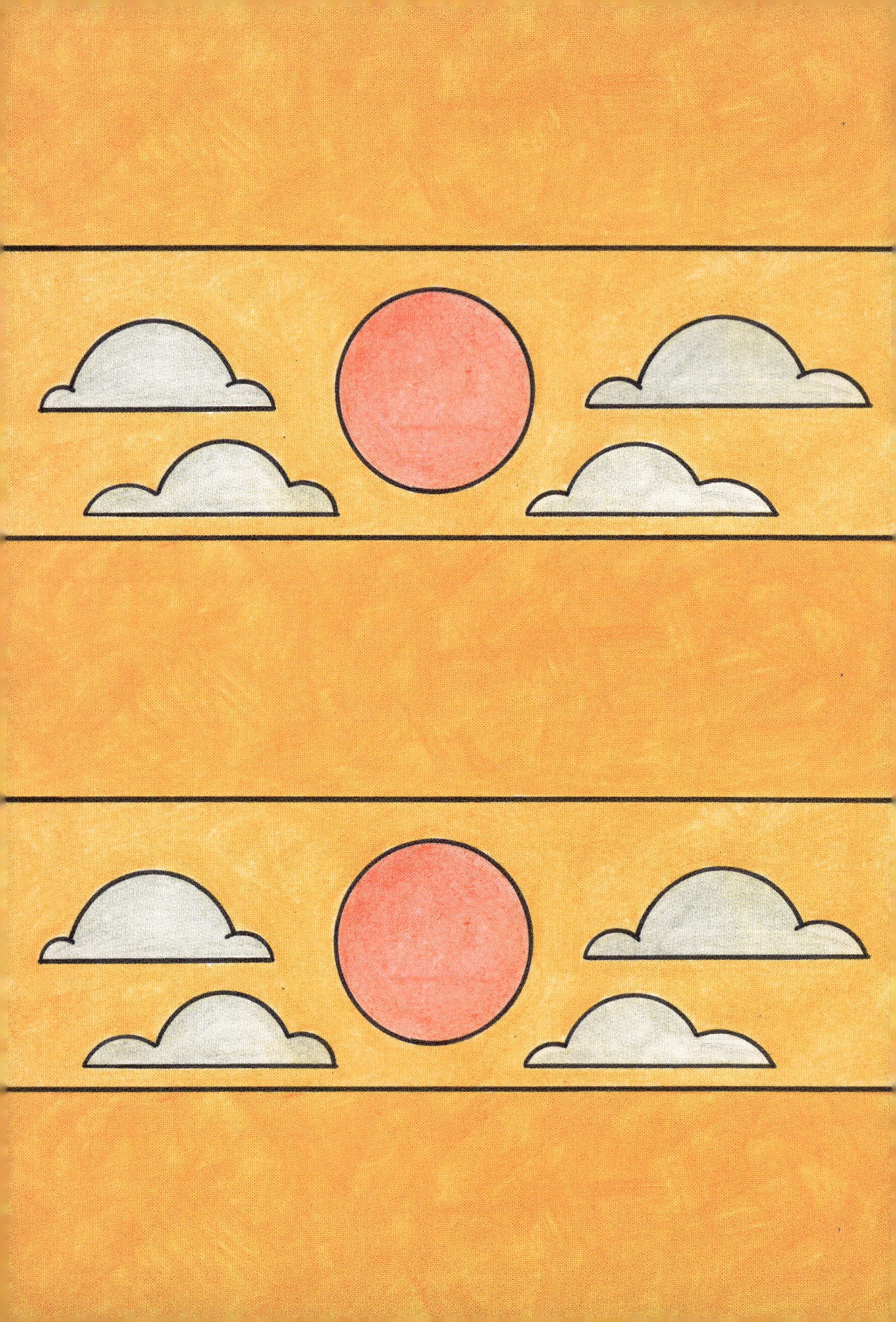

Chapter 8:
Aboriginal architecture today

Aboriginal people's lifestyles changed dramatically as a result of colonisation. No longer free to manage their clan estates, or stay connected with their ancestral lands and communities, or exchange stories and knowledge of Country with other groups, many people experienced the trauma of removal and disconnection and permanent resettlement on the fringes of the British colonisers' new towns and cities.

As fringe dwellers and residents in remote communities, suburbs, towns and cities across Australia, many Aboriginal people today still experience intergenerational trauma and a sense of loss and disconnection from Country. Loss of Country and loss of identity are two of the reasons why people feel they have to take back control of the decisions made over their lives.

And one of the ways to do this is to themselves become the architects, designers, town planners, teachers, doctors, lawyers and community leaders. It is about giving back the voice to Aboriginal people so they can also take particular care of their own people's needs.

Alison says

I am from La Perouse, close to where Captain Cook landed in south-east Sydney, which is ground zero for the colonial destruction of our Indigenous culture and way of life. I am learning more every day, working with Aboriginal Knowledge Holders and communities that design places and spaces, from a house to a whole city, that the things we make and build can be an extension of Country.

Undoing colonial design and town planning

The British colonists blanketed Aboriginal lands with their values by copying the buildings and landscapes they made in England and Europe and placing them here. They placed layers of brick, concrete, steel and glass over the earth with little understanding of its need for its environmental and cultural care. They believed in dominating nature in their approach to architecture and planning. It can be seen in the grid layouts of towns and cities across Australia, the landscapes that have become streetscapes, bare parks with formal rose gardens and stone monuments, the buildings that turn their back on rivers and the roads that cover the creeks.

But there is a way forward and that is to take the built environment as another kind of code for Country. The design of new places and spaces can also create meaning that talks to some of the traditional values that have been lost and reminds us that these are places and spaces that are part of the Dreaming and have an ancient history. This also starts with the renaming of special places. Have you been to the new suburb of Barangaroo in Sydney?

Barangaroo

The name from this suburb comes from Barangaroo, who was a strong Cammeraygal woman married to Bennelong, the well-known ambassador between the Aboriginal people and the British. She was a skilful fisher who provided her clan with fish and other seafoods. She took on the role, like many Aboriginal women, in controlling the food supply, so she was an important community leader and Elder.

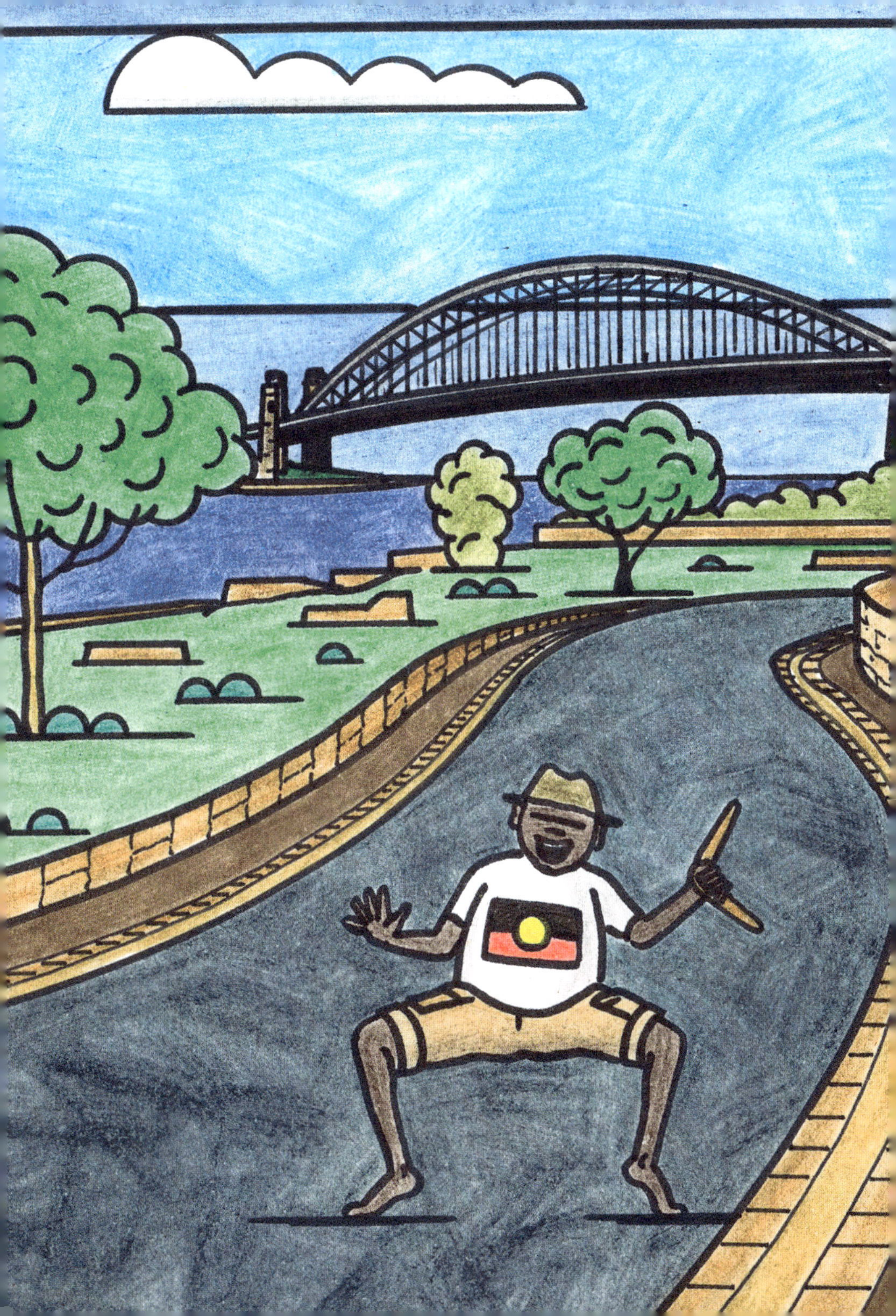

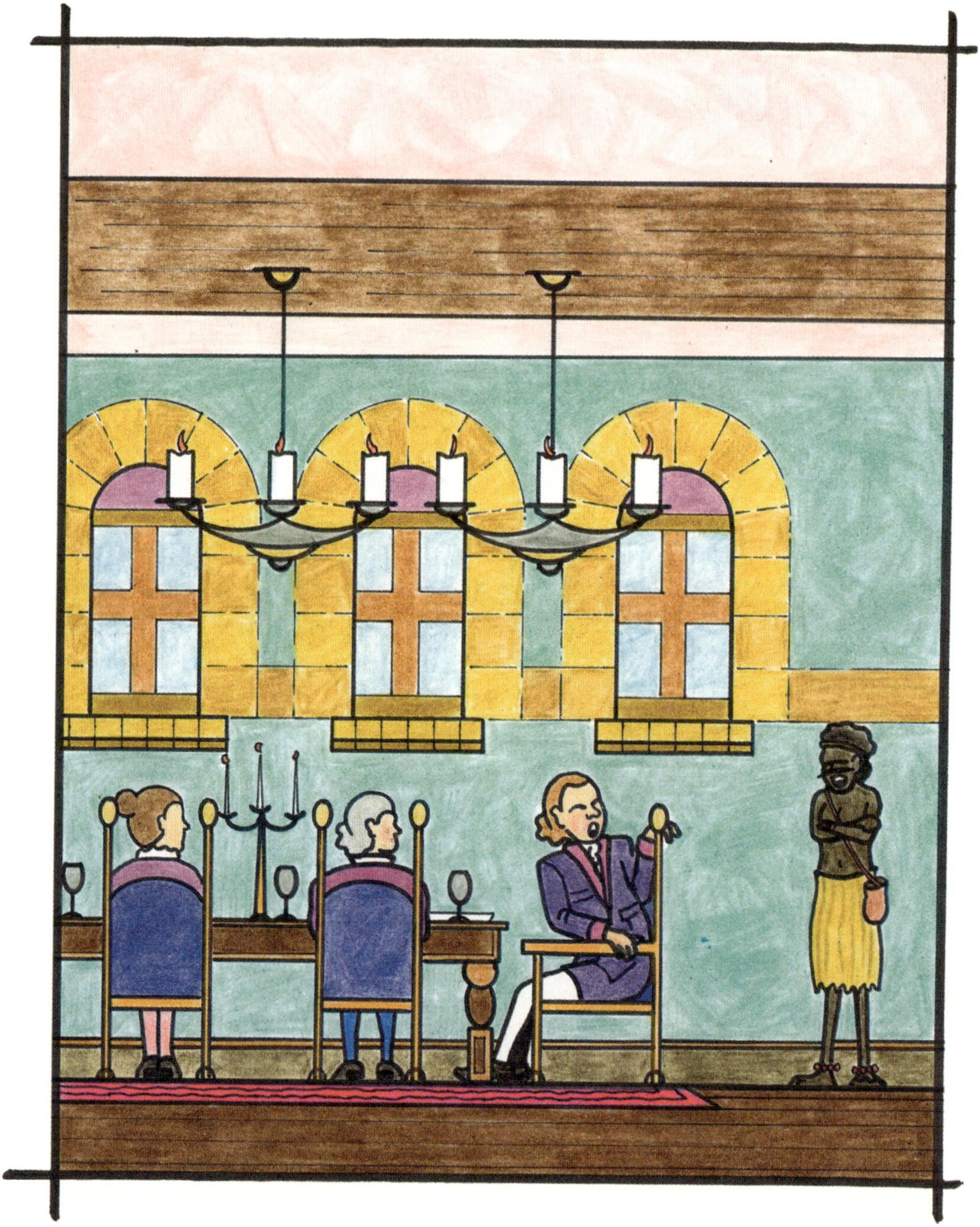

Alison says

Barangaroo and Bennelong first met the white people on the north shore at Kirribilli in 1790. This meeting was at the same time that the colonists netted some 4,000 Australian salmon from Sydney Harbour, and they sent forty fish over to Bennelong's group as a gift. Barangaroo was very angry at this excessively large catch of fish. She also criticised the British for the way that they treated the convict labourers so harshly. She wasn't going to just look away like Bennelong did to keep up positive relations. She turned up at the official dinner at the governor's house in traditional ornaments and grass skirt with a bone in her nose, but no other clothes because she refused to dress like the colonists.

She is no doubt an important figure in the history of Australia, which is why a large development on Sydney Harbour was recently named after her. This place on the western side of Walsh Bay was where her people camped on a large headland adjacent to the deepest part of the harbour, which would have been great for fishing. Over the years, the maritime industry and its demands of loading and unloading ships flattened the headland until the whole area was a large concrete slab.

In 2006, a plan was approved to rebuild the headland, plant endemic species, reinstate the shoreline and even make a cove safe for swimming. That is what our people call 'rematriating' Country, which, like objects, is about returning Country to the people. It is a way of connecting to Country in a city, and I reckon Barangaroo would be pretty proud to have this place named after her.

Rethinking Aboriginal housing

There are still a lot of problems caused in the last 250 years we need to fix. The poor standards of official Australian Government Aboriginal housing and housing policy have been problems since at least the 1950s, and it still is in many regional and remote communities. But some of the best housing solutions come from Aboriginal people themselves. They go back to the history of town camp settlements, when Aboriginal peoples had to adapt to settlement life and make the best of it.

Aboriginal people used whatever materials they could find to build town camps, including iron sheeting, wire, fencing posts, canvas, timber, plastic and metal utensils. With a few simple hand tools, sheets of iron could be cut, bent, folded and reshaped to fit. Like the sheets of bark that were used in traditional camps, flat or skillion (sloped) roofs made of metal or shade cloth were a common design feature, as were multiple campfires, windbreaks and outdoor sleeping arrangements. The camps had covered spaces for food and equipment, drums full of drinking water, fire roasting pits and garage spaces where people fixed up their old cars.

The camps were set up to suit big extended families and communities doing their work, raising children and going away for extended periods of time to revisit Country.

Family and kinship

Officers of the New South Wales Department of Housing in Wilcannia tried to get people out of town camps and into town housing estates, but they couldn't understand why their Aboriginal clients weren't taking up the housing offered to them. They allocated the houses to people as they became available following their usual assessment criteria and what we today call the 'salt and pepper policy' of alternating white and black households across the community. It took many rejections from their Aboriginal clients before the government realised that people would only accept houses offered to them if they were close to their families and kinship networks.

Alison says

Most Aboriginal housing in regional and remote communities today has not been designed and built by Aboriginal people. And it shows. They are hot, overcrowded and boring-looking boxes that look like they just landed there, with nothing to do with the Country around them. They are like the worst kind of cheap housing that got taken from the suburb of a city and placed without song or ceremony on Aboriginal land.

Some of the best Aboriginal houses are the ones that Aboriginal people made for themselves, and sometimes they aren't really houses at all – but a combination of traditional old-style shelters made with a range of old and new materials.

I have seen some great examples of this in my travels to remote communities where people get creative with the type of housing provided. I have seen modern versions of the old-style Aboriginal huts, which some people call a 'humpy', a 'wurley' or a 'gunya', built in people's front yards that are often more comfortable than the houses. People moved their lounge furniture into the huts and ran extension cords from the house to power their hi-fi systems, fridges and television sets. Sitting outside with their wider circle of friends and family, they seemed to be enjoying the best of both worlds.

Paul says

The design and layout of these town camps or fringe camps that Aboriginal people built for themselves in the 20th century provide useful models for the way to design community housing and other services. This includes making good use of outdoor spaces to allow people to move freely between their different indoor and outdoor settings.

Some Aboriginal master builders did come up with low-cost models for Aboriginal clients in the 1970s and 1980s. These were more comfortable and improved humpies with concrete floor slabs, carpets, curtains and air-conditioning units powered by generators. They could also be designed as modular houses, adding more and more rooms as needed.

But these kinds of buildings often didn't get approval from councils and other government bodies. It is only now that mainstream society is building small, temporary houses that more people can see the value of some of these Aboriginal-led housing projects.

Rebuilding trust in public institutions

Australia's poor track record of disconnection and separating Aboriginal families and communities has made many Aboriginal and Torres Strait Islander people distrust professionals for good reason. The way we build community facilities like schools, health clinics, hospitals and legal and court services now needs to be more user-friendly and responsive to the intergenerational trauma and cultural priorities of some Aboriginal people. We need to make sure that people don't feel trapped inside a building, or isolated from their community and familiar surroundings, with good visual access to the outside trees and landscape as well as to sun, light and air.

Where possible, the design of community buildings should also have cultural and symbolic value for the community. The building should speak to the Country on which it is built.

Alison says

When I joined Merrima Design, the Aboriginal design unit in the New South Wales Government Architect's Office, we came up with some great designs for community buildings. These included a hospital at Wilcannia that I worked on with Kevin O'Brien, a member of the Kaurareg and Meriam peoples from the Torres Strait, and Dillon Kombumerri, a member of the Yugambeh people from the Gold Coast, who was the principal architect.

At Wilcannia, the hospital was attached to an old colonial stone building, which turned its back on the river. We worked with the local Barkandji Elders, who led the community consultation process. Understandably, for a hospital, they wanted to promote health and wellbeing. They also wanted the building to mean something in connection with the river of their ancestral totem, Pardi the river cod.

So, the architecture started to take on the language of their totem, which was also environmentally responsive to Country. The walls and roof wrapped around the building like a skin and the windows were the gills of the fish. The building was made of stabilised earth bricks (from Country) and lightweight materials that allowed the free movement of air through the building.

Other necessary features included a mortuary. The community didn't want this to be too close to the people sleeping inside but the Health Department said it had to be part of the building. The solution was to provide a separate pavilion connected by a covered walkway. A campground was also provided next to the pavilion where communities could stay for months to conduct their 'Sorry Business', mourning the deceased.

The view from the hospital bed

How do you encourage Aboriginal clients to make use of hospital and health clinics? This is another important question to consider when designing buildings for medical services. It came up in a community consultation for the design of hospitals in Townsville and Mount Isa. The goal was to make hospitals more welcoming for Aboriginal people to get better health outcomes.

The design solution that the architecture and design team came up with was to design more comfortable entry, waiting and visitor access spaces at the hospital. They also recommended more visible connection to Country, so to encourage Aboriginal people to stay in hospital, they were given a room with a view.

The role of the Aboriginal architect

The Aboriginal architect is not just a lead designer. They are also the cultural content provider driving the approval and consultancy process with the Aboriginal community who are a part of the client group. The architect makes sure that all the important cultural protocols are communicated to the team of design and construction professionals. They bring together traditional knowledges and Western technology. That's why it is important for the project to be Aboriginal led and co-designed!

125

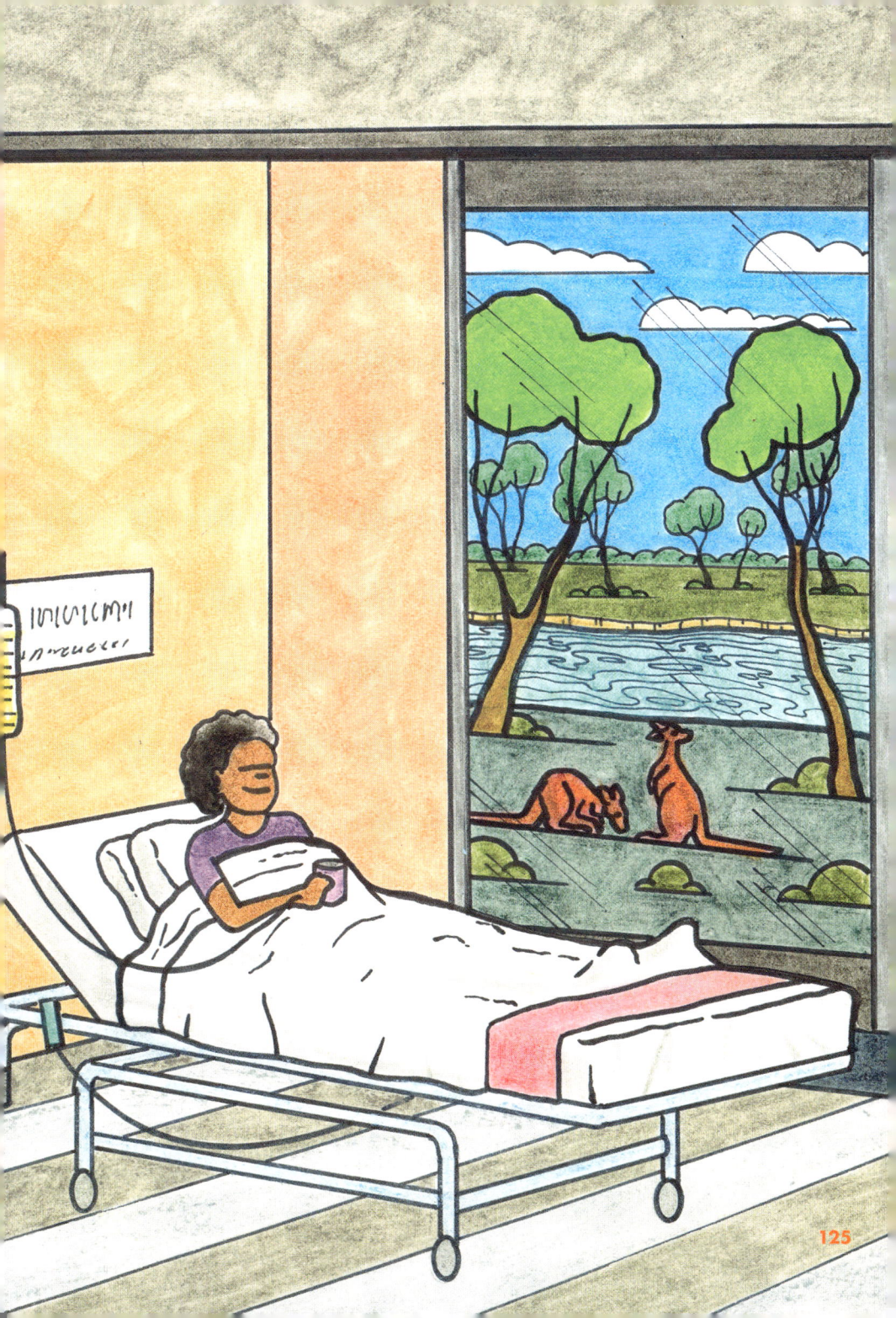

A definition of Aboriginal architecture

Aboriginal architecture is a way of turning buildings into story spaces that connect people and communities to Country, just like the Songlines that reach across the continent.

Big building projects involve many different building, design and construction professionals. But for buildings that we call Aboriginal architecture, Indigenous storytelling and traditional knowledge has to be central to the design process from the very start.

Each site, from a quarter-acre block to a large-scale inner city development, has different needs in terms of the mix of Indigenous people involved, but a project should always start with a conversation between the First Nations architects, landscape architects and designers and the story of Country.

The ideal production team includes ecologists, artists, curators and designers working with architects and landscape architects. As many as possible should be Indigenous, working with the Traditional Custodians and all contributing to the interpretation of what place-making architecture means today.

Aboriginal architecture today takes the principles of our traditional buildings and campsites and applies them to the design of new spaces and places. This architecture comes from a process where all the decisions that make a project successful respect Country and the memory of place and engage with the Traditional Custodians who will care for it.

First Nations architects are moving into new territory where they are bringing together the needs of the client and the functional requirements of the buildings with the needs of Country and the unique stories of place.

The global movement in Aboriginal architecture and design

All over the world First Nations peoples are telling us that the old ways are the new ways. They are telling anyone who wants to know about a new approach to design and architecture that brings Indigenous storytelling and traditional values to the built environment to support the needs of Indigenous communities today and their histories of place. The goal is to focus on the connection between people and culture and the environment, and to make people feel safe where they live, work and socialise. But most importantly, it is necessary to draw from the sustainability lessons of the old ways, whereby Country is respected and projects don't make climate change worse.

It is a way of also showing respect for the First Peoples of the world and honouring their creation stories. It is about survival into the future as well. There is a whole group of Indigenous architects and designers all over the world who are giving voice to their traditional knowledges by embedding it in the design of objects, buildings and even whole cities. And the world is ready to listen!

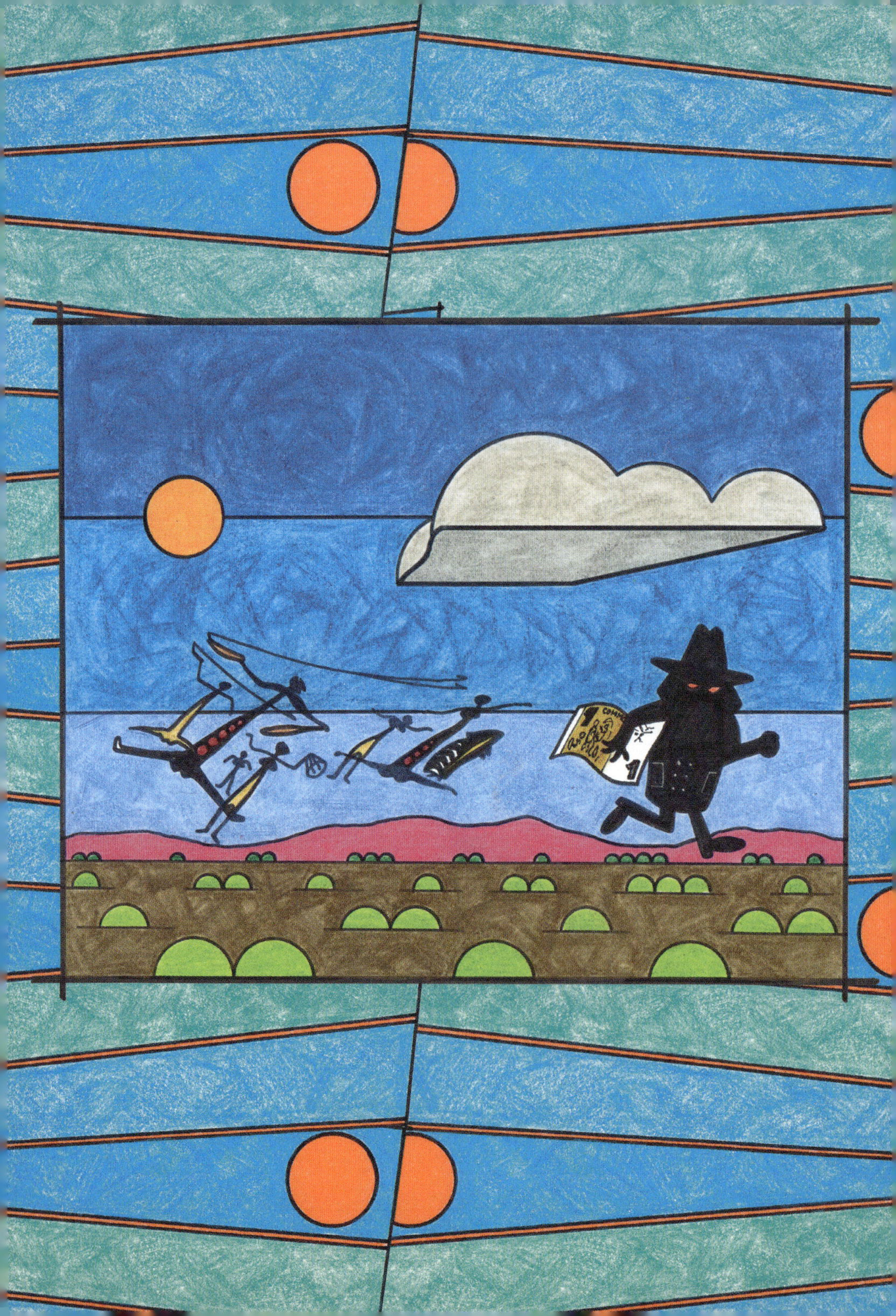

Chapter 9:
Design futures

When David Malangi Daymirringu's painting *Mortuary Feast of Gurrmirringu, the Great Ancestral Hunter* was used for the 1964 one dollar note, he was never approached for permission, awarded copyright payment or even given the opportunity to suggest a more suitable design for this use.

Aboriginal people weren't even counted in the Australian Census until several years later (after the successful 1967 Commonwealth Referendum).

It is one of many stories where Aboriginal and Torres Strait Islander peoples' culture and stories have been stolen to make products for sale by big companies.

In 2022, a very important collaboration between an Australian design company, Breville, and a group of Aboriginal artists set out to fix that. Called *An Aboriginal Culinary Journey*, the project saw the creation of appliances that were wrapped in artworks by artists Yalti and Yukultji Napangati and Warlimpirrnga Tjapaltjarri from Kiwirrkurra in Western Australia and Lucy Simpson, based in Sydney. They painted onto the coffee machine, toaster, kettle, oven and juicer in the same way their ancestors carved and etched stories onto their tools for living. The stories spoke of ancient Dreaming tracks, men's and women's ceremonies, ancient grains and medicine. To them, whether painting on the sand, a cave wall, their bodies or appliances, it is all about recording and remembering their Dreaming. Breville had to carefully scan the hand-painted objects and apply decals by hand to each one of the finished pieces. That's a lot of work!

For sale in Bloomingdale's New York and Harrods in London, the artists are paid a royalty for the sale of each piece and Breville are donating 100 per cent of the profits to an Aboriginal kindergarten, to the support of Aboriginal kids becoming top chefs and to the creation of the Institute for Designing with Country at the University of Technology, Sydney. That's the way we need to do our cultural business in the modern world!

And the world is loving this new way to tell our ancient stories. We are seeing an increasing number of Indigenous designers recognised at Paris Fashion Week, like Bobbi Lockyer, a Ngarluma, Kariyarra, Yawuru NS, Nyulnyul artist. And 2023 saw Denni Francisco of Indigenous clothing label Ngali have the first stand-alone show for an Indigenous designer in Australian Fashion Week's 23-year history.

All of these artists and their cultural expressions come from a place of respect for the importance of their Country, your Country and ours.

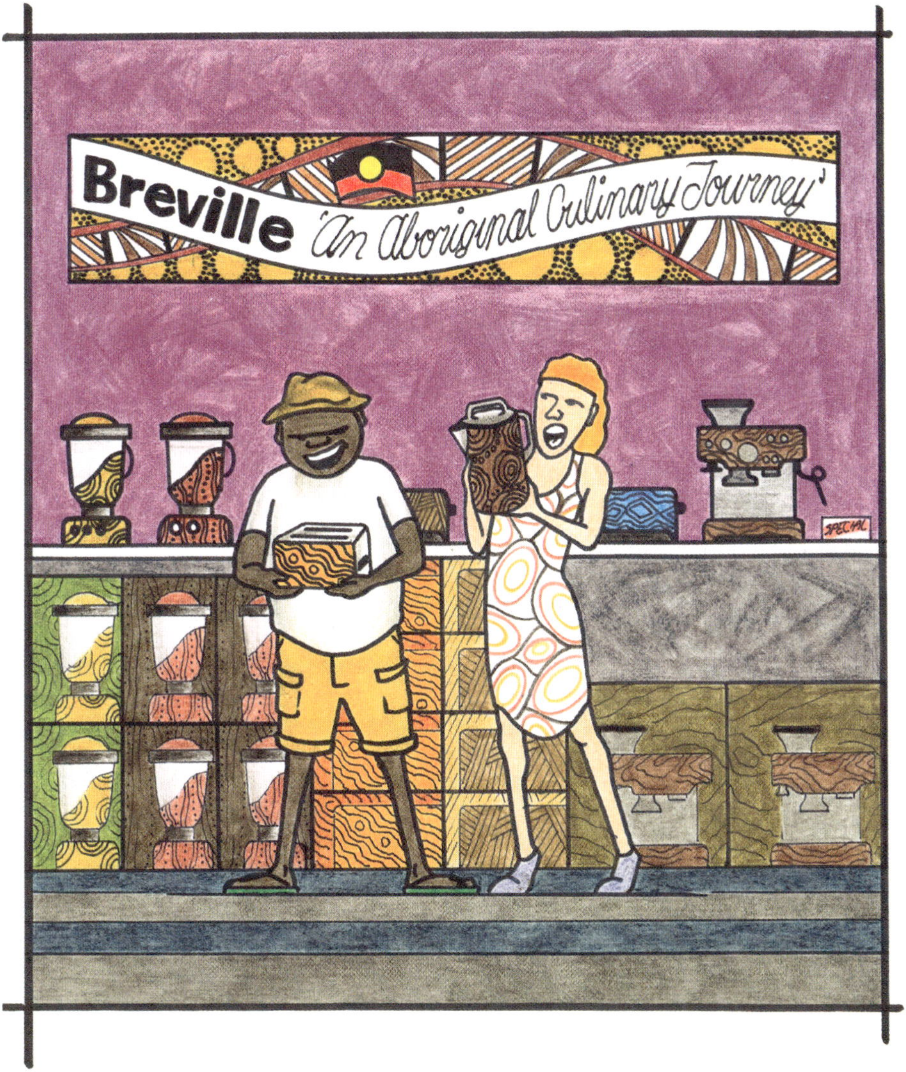
Breville
'An Aboriginal Culinary Journey'
SPECIAL

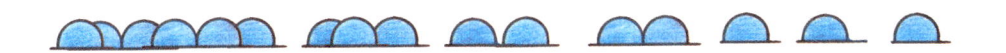

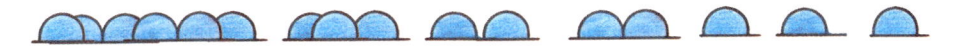

Finding Country means that you will see Australia in the same way. You will see yourself and what you do as part of the managed and sustainable way of life that allowed Aboriginal and Torres Strait Islander people to live successfully on this continent for millennia. It means a new way of working, relating, communicating and problem solving that considers *all* life, including our human and non-human kin: plants, animals, water and air. It means respecting the memory of place and its energy, from deep-time ancestral Dreaming tracks and Songlines to our contemporary and shared (sometimes painful) histories.

This is about designing objects, buildings and cities that are of *this* place. It is a generous invitation from our First Nations peoples to understand the stories of this land, to embed them into the things we make and build and continue a tradition of Australian design that started over 65,000 years ago. It is about designing a future where we can *all* belong to Country.

133

Your turn

OBJECTS FROM COUNTRY

Next time you go to a museum, look for traditional Aboriginal tools and objects (in museum language, these are called artefacts). Read the label to find out as much as you can about the objects and the materials used. See if you can locate the Country that it comes from on a map.

BUILDING WITH BARK

Look for photos and botanical descriptions of bark used for traditional bark shelters. Try to find out the difference between different types of bark. Where do they grow in Australia? Can you try to build one yourself?

WHAT'S IN YOUR BACKYARD?

Explore your backyard to see what natural materials you can find. Imagine if you had to survive using just these materials. What are some things you could make?

NATIVE FOODS

Do you know what native foods grow where you live? Look up a seasonal native food calendar for your region and think about this the next time you eat a meal. Can you think of some recipes to cook using native produce?

IMPORTANT OBJECTS

Ask a family member or friend about an object that is important to them. Is there a story that makes the object special?

CARING FOR COUNTRY

Do you or your family have places you visit that have special meaning to you? Draw one of these places and present it to your classmates.

CAMPING OUT

Have you ever gone camping or stayed overnight for a school excursion? Think about the camp layout. How was it organised? Can you draw it? Can you think of any ways to improve the design?

FIRST NATIONS' BUILDINGS

Research and visit (if appropriate) a First Nations designed public building or space. What do you notice? Is it different to what you expected? Why?

About the creators

Alison Page

Alison Page is a descendant of the Walbanga and Wadi Wadi people of the Dharawal and Yuin Nations and an award-winning artist whose work over twenty-five years promotes the creative expression of Aboriginal identity in public art, design and film. In 2015, Alison was inducted into the Design Institute of Australia's Hall of Fame. She appeared for eight years as a regular panelist on the ABC TV show *The New Inventors* and was the founder of Saltwater Freshwater Arts Alliance and the National Aboriginal Design Agency. Alison is an Associate Dean (Indigenous) at the Design, Architecture and Building Faculty at the University of Technology Sydney, a Councillor for the Australian National Maritime Museum and a Director with the National Australia Day Council.

Paul Memmott

Professor Paul Memmott AO is an anthropologist and architect. He founded the Aboriginal Environments Research Centre at the University of Queensland (School of Architecture and Institute for Social Science Research), where he has been Director for several decades. His research interests encompass Aboriginal sustainable housing and settlement design, Aboriginal access to institutional architecture, Indigenous constructs of place and cultural heritage, vernacular architecture, social planning in Indigenous communities, cultural change and architectural anthropology. Memmott also has extensive professional anthropological experience in Aboriginal land rights claims and Native Title claims.

Blak Douglas

Blak Douglas is a modern artist with proud Dhungutti Aboriginal origins. His works are culturally and politically charged with a sense of irony, parody and truth.

Blak is a trained illustrator and designer, and a self-taught painter. He won the 2018 Kilgour Prize, the 2020 STILL award and the 2022 Archibald Prize. His works are collected by the National Gallery of Australia, the Art Gallery of New South Wales, Queensland Art Gallery of Modern Art, the Australian National Maritime Museum, the National Museum of Australia, AIATSIS and other galleries in Australia and abroad.

Important words and concepts

Aboriginal and Torres Strait Islander people: the first peoples of Australia, also called First Nations peoples. Although there are hundreds of different groups with their own languages, histories and customs, all of them were impacted by colonisation.

aerofoil: a shaped form designed to help lift or control an aircraft or sailing boat. It does this by using the currents of air around it. For example, a jet aeroplane wing is in the shape of an aerofoil.

anthropologist: someone who studies the way of life of a group of people, how their way of life developed, their customs, values and beliefs. Anthropologists discover this information by living with that group of people and by exploring their culture, language and evolution pattern.

archaeologist: someone who studies the customs and behaviours of groups of people, especially prehistoric cultures, by carefully digging up and examining their remains.

clan estates: each group of people associated with an Ancestral being or a totem was known as a clan. The clan estate was the land they were responsible for.

colonisation: when the British people first came to Australia and forced many First Nations people off their ancestral lands, and killed many as well. Taking the land destroyed a lot of First Nations cultures, threatening their survival, and in many cases causing their extinction.

intergenerational trauma: when communities and individuals have not had the opportunity to heal from past traumatic experiences the effects are passed down through generations. This can result in disconnection from extended families, feeling stressed or difficulties with nurturing relationships.

kinship: a structure of relationships based on bloodline descent and marriage that helps a person find where they fit in their community. This tells them the role they should have and the way to communicate with others.

missions and reserves: sections of land, usually on the outskirts or fringes of towns, where Aboriginal and Torres Strait Islander peoples were forced to live. Many aspects of their lives were controlled, including money, relationships, religion and what language was spoken. Missions were usually established and run by churches and reserves were usually under the control of the government.

mob: a group of Aboriginal or Torres Strait Islander people associated with a particular place or Country. It can represent a family group, clan group, or wider community or Nation. It is a common way Aboriginal and Torres Strait Islander people refer to their family and their people but is not appropriate for non-Indigenous people to use without permission.

rematriating: re-establishing and restoring sacred relationships between First Nations people and their Ancestral Lands, and returning Country to First Peoples. It can also mean returning objects back to their homelands or communities. It is sometimes called repatriation.

'salt and pepper' policy: a term for a housing policy where Aboriginal and Torres Strait Islander peoples were housed alongside non-Indigenous residents to mix up the families in the street. The aim was to disconnect them from their own culture and force them into colonial society.

saltwater and freshwater people: the elements of the nature around a group of Aboriginal people defines their Dreamings and what they do on Country. Saltwater and freshwater people come from areas near water and specify what kind of water.

Sorry Business: a period of mourning with Aboriginal or Torres Strait Islander cultural practices that takes place after someone's death, usually carried out as a community.

Index

Aboriginal architecture 111–13, 118–27
An Aboriginal Culinary Journey 129–30
Aboriginal designers 129–30
Aboriginal housing 118–21
Aboriginal Nations 2, 4–5, 91
Ancestors 2, 14–15
Ancestral Beings 10–11, 12–13, 40, 60, 82, 87
architecture 111–13, 118–27
Australian Fashion Week 130
Australian Museum 22
axes 52

Barangaroo 114, 117
bark 29–30
bark buckets 68–9
Barkandji people 86, 123
baskets and containers 68–9, 71
Bennelong 117
bicornual baskets 69, 71
black wattle trees 25
boomerangs 22, 26, 42, 45, 48–50, 53, 63, 79–80
bread 66
Breville 129–30
Brewarrina fish traps 82
bull kelp containers 68

campsites 91–101, 118
ceremonies 16, 37, 50, 57, 60
clubs 63
colonists 29, 32, 33, 51–2, 84, 108, 111, 113
community buildings 122–3
connection, to Country 6–7, 19, 28
coolamons 42, 60, 71

Country 1–17, 19–20, 24, 32–3, 37, 44, 45, 99, 101, 108, 111, 132

dancing 57
Daymirringu, David Malagi 129
demountable buildings 104
desert people 33, 45
Dharawal people 47
dilly bags 71
The Dreaming 10–11, 26, 38, 54, 97, 99

Elders 7, 26, 42, 98–9, 101, 114, 123
emus 84

family and kinship 7, 119
farming practices 81
fashion 130
feasts 57, 59
fibre technologies 88, 107
fire 73, 75, 97
firestick farming 61, 73
fish traps 16, 30, 81–7
fishing 16, 50, 51, 61, 64, 81–7
food 33, 57, 59–66
Francisco, Denni 130

glass 54
grains 64
grinding stones 72
Gurrmanamana, Frank 16
Gweagal people 47

harpoons 63
hospitals 123, 124
housing 118–21
hunting 45, 57, 63, 84

identity, loss of 111
Indjilandi people 41–2

Jacob, Jackson 22
Jaurth, Fred 98–9

Kaiadilt people 87
kangaroos 84
kitchen tools 68–9, 71–2
knives 38
knowledge of Country 1, 25, 66, 111
Konbumerri, Dillon 123

landcare practices 81
languages 10
Lardil people 32, 48, 50, 64, 84, 87, 98–9
Lockyer, Bobbi 130

Merrima Design 123
metal axes 52
middens 33
mortuaries 123
Mortuary Feast of Gurrmirringu (painting) 129

netting practices 61, 64, 84

objects, made on Country 14–15, 16, 40–1, 44
O'Brien, Kevin 123
obsidian 38
on Country 1
oral knowledge 8

painting 50, 63, 129
plant materials 25, 28–30, 103
public institutions, trust in 122
Pwerle, Colin Saltmere 42, 88

Rainbow Serpent 26
recycling 20, 55
red ochre 38
Referendum (1967) 129
rematriating, of Country 117
rock-wall fish traps 84–7

seeds 66
separation, from Country 32
shells 33, 35, 38
shelters 29, 93–4, 103–8, 118
shields 42, 47, 50
singing 16, 22, 50, 57
Songlines 8–9, 12, 45, 54
spears 38, 45, 47, 50, 54, 63
spinifex 30, 42, 88, 107
spirituality 22
stone tools 40–2, 52
stories 26–7, 82
string and twine 30, 32

tools 37–55, 68–9, 71–2
totems 10, 25, 45
town camps 119, 121
Traditional Owners 33, 35, 44, 53
trapping practices 16, 81–2, 84–7
Tubowgule 33, 35

Warlpiri people 50
wattle trees 25
weatherproof shelters 105
Wilcannia 119, 123
windbreaks 94–5, 96–7
wooden tools 44
woomeras 45, 47

X-ray art 63

Yir Yoront people 52

About the series

The First Knowledges for younger readers series is based on the award-winning adult books.

Songlines by Margo Neale and Lynne Kelly

Design & Building on Country by Alison Page and Paul Memmott

Caring for Country by Bill Gammage and Bruce Pascoe will be published in 2025.